Falconry
AT THE UNITED STATES AIR FORCE ACADEMY

The Story of the Cadets' Unique Performing Mascot

A. P. Clark
Lieutenant General, USAF (Ret.)

The Friends of the United States Air Force Academy Library
and

Fulcrum Publishing
Golden, Colorado

Copyright © 2003 The Friends of the Air Force Academy Library

All rights reserved. No part of this book may be reproduced, stored in a retrieval system, or transmitted in any form or by any means, electronic, mechanical, photocopying, recording, or otherwise, without written permission from the publisher.

Library of Congress Cataloging-in-Publication Data

Clark, A. P. (Albert Patton), 1913–
   Falconry at the United States Air Force Academy : the story of the cadets' unique performing mascot / A.P. Clark.
     p. cm.
Includes bibliographical references (p.).
   ISBN 1-55591-487-X (paperback : alk. paper)
   ISBN 1-55591-497-7 (hardcover : alk. paper)
  1. Falconry—Colorado—Colorado Springs. 2. United States Air Force Academy—Mascots. I. Title.
SK321.C58 2003
799.2'32'0978856—dc21

2002152606

Printed in China

0 9 8 7 6 5 4 3 2 1

Jacket and interior design by Patty Maher
Cover image: Courtesy Special Collections, Air Force Academy Library.
Back cover image: Aurora, the gyrfalcon mascot of the United States Air Force Academy, shown in 2001. Photo by Master Sergeant Kenneth L. Carter, courtesy Special Collections of the Air Force Academy Library.

Fulcrum Publishing
16100 Table Mountain Parkway, Suite 300
Golden, Colorado 80403
(800) 992-2908 • (303) 277-1623
www.fulcrum-books.com

Contents

Foreword • vii
   by Dr. Harold M. Webster
Introduction and Acknowledgments • ix
The Friends of the United States Air Force Academy Library • xi
The Ancient Sport of Falconry • 1
The Types of North American Falcons • 3

Falcons at the Air Force Academy • 7
   Choosing a Mascot • 9
   The Academy Acquires Its Falcons • 13
   Assistance from Individuals and Groups • 19
   Facilities and Equipment • 23
   Breeding Falcons in Captivity • 27
   Feeding the Falcons • 31
   Contributions to the Art and Science of Falconry • 33

The Cadets and Their Falcons • 35
   Organization of the Falconry Program • 37
   Falcon Handler Training • 41
   Training the Performing Mascots • 47
   Public Affairs • 55
   Conclusion • 59

Appendices • 61
   Officers-in-Charge/Directors of the Academy Falconry Program • 63
   Roster of First Class Cadet Falcon Handlers, 1959–2003 • 65
   Glossary • 69
   Academy Library Resources and Select Bibliography • 75
   Index • 81

Reprinted from *Falconers' Favorites,* 1865.

Foreword

To have had an active role in the introduction of the falcon as the new mascot of the United States Air Force Academy was truly a dream come true. Everyone in the state of Colorado was anxiously awaiting the opening of the newest service academy on a magnificent, pine-covered site at the foot of the Rocky Mountains between Denver and Colorado Springs. The construction plans called for establishing a campus that would be one of the finest in the world, and certainly a highly rated tourist attraction. Its opening would be the most exciting event to take place in Colorado for years.

As a practicing falconer I was well acquainted with resident, nesting prairie falcons (*Falco mexicanus*) that lived on the new Air Force Academy grounds. Announcements reached the press that officials of the Academy were searching for a suitable mascot. It was quite obvious that a falcon would be an appropriate choice—an avian speedster of unparalleled aerial superiority, and a species completely dominating the skies. Once the cadets were introduced to what a falcon might do in the air, their vote established the choice of a mascot.

Lt. Gen. Hubert R. Harmon, the first Superintendent, was thrilled with the choice of the falcon, and it was my privilege and honor to assist the Academy for several years in their falcon mascot project. We went all over the globe bringing home specimens that were used by the Cadet Wing for display as well as for mascots. Assisting the Air Force Academy gave this old Navy man a unique opportunity. I was afforded excellent cooperation by both the academic staff and the student body. Their approach to the many problems encountered in the care and management of a team of avian fighters that would show their abilities at halftime during football games throughout the United States was a credit to the Academy.

I salute you, the United States Air Force Academy.

Dr. Harold M. Webster
LCdr, USNR (Ret.)

Dr. Harold M. Webster, distinguished national falconer and author.
Photo courtesy Dr. Harold Webster.

U.S. Air Force F-16 *Fighting Falcon* aircraft with gyrfalcon. Image courtesy Wildlife Internationale, Inc.

Introduction and Acknowledgments

The falconry program at the United States Air Force Academy has generated many inquiries and has intrigued countless visitors for years. These beautiful, alert, and fierce-looking birds of prey, or raptors, flying free in demonstrations or perched calmly on the fists of their cadet handlers, seem to epitomize the mission and spirit of the United States Air Force and its Academy.

This little book tells how the Academy's unique falconry program came to exist and describes the imaginative and innovative work that has produced this exciting application of an ancient sport. For centuries eagles, hawks, and falcons have been trained by man to hunt. At the Academy, falcons are trained to fly free over stadiums filled with thousands of people and to perform thrilling aerial maneuvers—stoops and dives in recognizable simulation of the more spectacular aspects of the mission of the United States Air Force.

During the more than forty years of the Academy program's development, the art of falconry and the meticulous aspects of the handling of these birds—their breeding and feeding, their care and training—have been significantly advanced. Of equal importance, the cooperative way that the new knowledge and techniques have been shared with numerous local and national falconry organizations has gained recognition for the Air Force Academy and the respect everywhere of experts in the field. These are also important elements of the story that unfolds in the following pages.

☆ ☆ ☆

No one puts together a book like this without lots of help. I am most indebted to an official report on the Academy falconry program submitted in 1995 by Colonel Lawrence E. Schaad at the end of his distinguished service as the program's director. I, along with The Friends of the Air Force Academy Library, also particularly appreciate the financial support provided by the Association of Graduates of the United States Air Force Academy. Among the many others who assisted with the book, the following deserve special thanks:

Major Mark J. Abbott, USAFR, a cadet falcon handler in the Class of 1983, provided a number of the photographs.

Master Sergeant Kenneth L. Carter, USAF, provided photographs and put all of the book's illustration on a CD.

Colonel Arthur O. Compton, ANG, a cadet falcon handler in the Class of 1972, provided photographs and assisted in research.

Colonel Elliott V. Converse, III, USAF (Ret.), served as principal editor.

Mrs. Wendy Corbett, who as Wendy K. Girton, Class of 1982, was the first female cadet falcon handler, provided photographs.

Charles Elms, a photographer with the Academy's 10th Communications Squadron, lent his skills to producing the book's illustrations.

Executive Committee, The Friends of the United States Air Force Academy Library, gave continuous support: **Brig. Gen. Philip D. Caine, USAF (Ret.); Brig. Gen. George V. Fagan, USAF (Ret.); Lt. Col. Dona R. H. Hildebrand, USAF (Ret.); Willis I. Ketterson; Col. Henry A. Kortemeyer, USAF (Ret.);** and **Col. Jock C. H. Schwank, USAF (Ret.).**

Michael J. Finley, a cadet falcon handler in the Class of 1983, assisted with research and photographs.

Captain Julie Krygier, USAF, a former assistant director of the falconry program, reviewed the manuscript, made many helpful suggestions, and provided photographs.

Gertrude Pollok, of the Academy Library's Special Collections staff, supplied many hours of editorial and typing assistance.

Duane J. Reed, the Air Force Academy archivist, offered valuable guidance and editorial assistance.

Lt. Col. James Riddle, USAF, a former falconry program director, reviewed the manuscript and offered excellent advice.

Dr. Edward A. Scott, Director of Academy Libraries, enthusiastically supported publication of the volume.

Major Nathan K. Watanabe, USA, a cadet falcon handler in the Class of 1988, assisted in research and provided photographs.

Major Timothy Woodruff, USAF, director of the Academy falconry program from July 1999 to July 2002, reviewed the manuscript and arranged for important photographs of the cadet handlers and their birds.

Hunting with falcons. Reprinted from the book *Fauconnerie: Catalogue Illustre.* Paris, 1890.

The Friends of the United States Air Force Academy Library

The Friends of the United States Air Force Academy Library is a tax-exempt charitable foundation established in 1987 to enhance the quality of the Academy Library as an educational, research, scientific, and cultural institution. The Friends enable the library to acquire materials, to pursue projects, to create publications, and to implement services beyond those made possible through funds allocated by the United States Air Force.

The Friends sponsored this account of the Academy's falconry program to fulfill requests expressed many times by Academy personnel and by the school's friends and visitors to know more about the falcons and their cadet handlers. Lt. Gen. A. P. Clark, the book's author and also the Academy's sixth superintendent, received help and encouragement from many but especially from those who participated in the falconry program during its nearly half-century history.

Falconry in ancient Arabia. Image courtesy Special Collections, Air Force Academy Library.

The Ancient Sport of Falconry

The Sport of Hunting. For thousands of years trained wild birds have been used in the sport of hunting. The most suitable proved to be the raptors—eagles, hawks, and falcons—birds with lethal, hooked beaks and large, strong feet with talons capable of gripping their quarry. Falconry, or hawking as the sport was called in early accounts, appears to have been first developed by nomadic peoples in Central Asia at a very early period of history. Falconry is also recorded as having been cultivated by the emperors of China in the seventh century B.C. and was practiced in Japan by the third century A.D. Additionally, historians tell us that falconry was familiar to the peoples of Persia and northern India by 400 B.C. How and when this sport reached western Asia, northern Africa, and Europe is lost to history but an account written in 336 A.D. describes falconry being practiced in Europe. By 500 A.D. the sport was well known in what is now France and engaged in by the kings of the Franks.

Through the Middle Ages the art of hunting with raptors was intimately associated with the well-born throughout Europe. In fact, for anyone who claimed to be of noble birth or wealthy family, knowledge of falconry was indispensable. All the countries of Europe enjoyed their own traditions of the sport and nowhere was it practiced with more splendor than in France.

The Arabs were also well advanced in the art of falconry; it flourished in Turkey, Egypt, and other parts of the Middle East by 800 A.D. The Crusaders brought Arab knowledge and experience back to Europe, further stimulating the practice there. When the Europeans voyaged west, Cortez and his men were amazed to discover that the Aztecs of Mexico, under Montezuma, were familiar with birds of prey and kept them but, as far as is known, did not hunt with them.

For centuries the knowledge and skills of falconry were passed down from generation to generation and reached a very high level of sophistication. Falconry was not an efficient way to hunt for food but was primarily a sport for those who could afford the facilities to house the birds, the entourage of helpers to care for them, the horses for the hunters to ride, and the dogs to locate the falcon's prey. For this reason falconry has been traditionally referred to as the "sport of kings." Sadly, when the age of kings ran its course much of falconry know-how was lost.

Flying to the Lure. At one time or another during the millennia that this sport has been practiced, falcons have also been trained to pursue an artificial lure as an exercise to prepare them to hunt wild quarry. Flying the falcon in this way very closely simulates the flight pattern the bird would make if it were actually hunting.

Cadets at the Air Force Academy have trained their birds to fly to the lure even when released to fly free over large, noisy stadium crowds. Although training falcons to attack a lure may have had precedent, the practice had to be learned anew by Academy cadets with the assistance of several experienced falconers who generously lent their time and skills to the task. The cadet handlers have managed to fly two birds to the same lure and to stage performances at night—both radical innovations. It was a challenge for the new cadet handlers to acquire these skills and to develop the patience necessary to make their falcons respond to this marked departure from the typical hunting scenario—an accomplishment much to their credit.

A cadet falconer flying his bird to the lure.
Photo courtesy Office of the Director of Falconry, Air Force Academy.

The Types of North American Falcons

There are five species of falcons and several species of hawks common to North America; all are frequently trained to hunt. Because of its striking beauty and grace, the falcon, for centuries in Europe and then in North America, came to be considered a more prestigious bird than the hawk. In addition, the first class to graduate from the Academy, the Class of 1959, felt that the speed, courage, and powerful flight of the falcon best represented the mission of the United States Air Force. For these reasons, the Air Force Academy chose the falcon as its mascot over the hawk and developed a unique and exciting falconry program.

Falcons are referred to by falconers as longwings largely to distinguish them from the hawks, called shortwings. The flight profiles of the two are significantly different. The North American falcons are, in the order of their average size, starting with the smallest: the **kestrel**, the **merlin**, the **prairie falcon**, the **peregrine**, and the **gyrfalcon**. The **aplomado** is native to Central and South America. The literature on its use by falconers is scant but some are bred in the United States; they will probably become more common among falconers if captive breeding and other efforts succeed in removing them from endangered status.

All of these birds share certain characteristics that set them apart from most other birds. Falcons possess keen eyesight—about six to eight times as acute as human sight. Their eyes are a dark brown, so dark they appear almost black. In contrast, hawks have yellow or reddish-colored eyes. Another distinguishing feature of the falcon is the stripe that runs from the eye down across its cheek. The stripe varies in prominence among the different species but is always present. A close look at the falcon's beak reveals another distinguishing characteristic. About halfway down the upper mandible is a small hook, or tooth, on the beak. The falcon's shape and posture is also unique. It has sharp, pointed wings that cross over behind the bird when the wings are at rest against the body.

Falcons are powerful and graceful in flight with strong, deep wing beats. They maneuver with ease, grace, and evident enjoyment. The sharp wing design allows for agile maneuverability but is not ideal for gliding. Therefore, a falcon in flight flaps its wings frequently except during its attack dive, or stoop. During the stoop, the falcon tucks its wings close to its body and gathers amazing speed as it plunges from above at its prey. Falcons have nictating membranes to protect their eyes and baffles in their nostrils to assure proper air intake during high-speed attacks on their prey. The stoop has earned the falcon a nickname from the cadet falconers—"The Feathered Missile." Falcons are very alert, stand with an almost regal carriage, and are fearless and aggressive especially in defense of their nest and young against intruders. They have been known to attack and to kill prey more than twice their size.

While not officially so designated, the **gyrfalcon,** the largest falcon, is generally accepted as the premiere Academy mascot. This noble bird's habitat is the far north, generally north of the tree line throughout the world. Gyrfalcons occur in a variety of graded plumage color phases—from white or near-white, flecked with gray, through black (varying in color from pale gray to a dark smoke gray), to a black so dark as to be almost indistinguishable from that of the raven. Throughout the long history of falconry, gyrfalcons, especially the white-phase variety, have been the most highly prized. They are the largest, the most beautiful, and the most capable.

The **peregrine** is also a large falcon. Both sexes look alike but the female (the falcon) is about one-third larger than the male (the tiercel). Peregrines are widely distributed around the world resulting in many populations and about twenty-two subspecies. The peregrine is an agile and efficient hunter and has been recorded in stoops at speeds of over 200 miles an hour. The Air Force Academy has bred, raised, and trained peregrines to perform from time to time but it is not preferred as a performer. In 1999, the peregrine was removed from the category of endangered species but is still being bred in captivity for release to the wild.

The **prairie falcon,** a medium-size falcon, is the bird most used at the Academy for flying demonstrations. The female prairie is larger than the male and both are performers, but the male is consistently the best. In the early days of the falconry program, peregrines and gyrfalcons were

Left: Glacier, a gyrfalcon and the Air Force Academy mascot from 1980 to 1995. Photo courtesy Maj. Nathan K. Watanabe, Class of 1988.

Right: A peregrine falcon. Photo courtesy Office of Public Affairs, Air Force Academy.

The Types of North American Falcons

Left: **A prairie falcon.** Photo courtesy Office of the Director of Falconry, Air Force Academy.

Right: **A kestrel falcon.** Photo courtesy Office of the Director of Falconry, Air Force Academy.

A merlin falcon. Photo courtesy Office of the Director of Falconry, Air Force Academy.

also trained to perform. Oddly, the prairie falcon, of all the larger falcons, has a reputation as being the most irascible and the least forgiving in its attitude toward its trainer. The Academy selected it anyway because of its easy availability.

The **merlin** is slightly larger than the kestrel, the smallest falcon. In the field merlins appear uniformly dark. Males, with slate-blue wings and back, appear brighter than the females, which are uniformly brown. Merlins are also found worldwide and often nest in urban areas. They feed on small birds but have been known to take pigeons larger than themselves.

The **kestrel** is not only the smallest falcon found in North America but also one of the most plentiful. Males have a rusty-colored back and tail and blue wings. In both sexes the top of the head is blue with a rusty cap. American kestrels are widely distributed throughout the Western Hemisphere. They feed on insects, small rodents, and birds.

FALCONS AT THE AIR FORCE ACADEMY

The Air Force Academy from the falcon's point of view.
Photo courtesy Special Collections, Air Force Academy Library.

Choosing a Mascot

The adoption of an animal or bird as a mascot by a collegiate institution has a long history. Usually the animal or bird selected possesses attributes or characteristics that students would like to emulate or perhaps has some historic association with the institution. For example, the Massachusetts Institute of Technology, known for its engineering curriculum, chose the beaver because of its skill in constructing dams, and the United States Military Academy chose the mule because of its long association with the U.S. Army. The United States Naval Academy apparently chose the goat as its mascot by accident. In 1890 the midshipmen, while en route by train to a football game, saw a goat during a short stop; somehow the goat joined the entourage through a practice commonly known as a "midnight requisition."

Early Proposals. Even before the first class was admitted, there was interest at the new Air Force Academy in adopting an appropriate mascot. In October 1954, Air Force Capt. Donald R. Galvin, in a letter to the Academy's first Superintendent, Lt. Gen. Hubert R. Harmon, proposed the falcon. In a radio address the following month, Brig. Gen. Woodbury Burgess, then Director of Intelligence, Air Defense Command, also recommended the falcon. A few months later Col. Russell L. Meredith, USAF (Ret.), a graduate of West Point, Class of 1917, a pioneer Army aviator and respected as the "Father of American Falconry" and President of the Falconry Club of America, also suggested to his friend General Harmon that the falcon be adopted as the Academy's mascot. As a result of these suggestions and correspondence with the Secretary of the Air Force, the Academy's Chief of Staff requested that the Commandant of Cadets study the matter and make recommendations concerning the selection of a mascot.

The Selection Process. Accordingly in May 1955, just two months before the first cadets arrived, Col. (later Brig. Gen.) Robert M.

Col. Russell "Luff" Meredith (1892–1965), the "Father of American Falconry," with *Kris*. Photo courtesy The Archives of American Falconry.

Stillman, Commandant of Cadets, appointed an ad hoc committee for this purpose. Both General Stillman and the committee believed the cadets themselves should select the mascot; it would be a one-time privilege for the first class of cadets scheduled to graduate in 1959. Thus the committee decided simply to make a recommendation and to leave the decision to the cadets.

The committee members first considered domestic animals, bearing in mind that they would be the easiest to care for, whereas a wild animal would have to be caged and would present problems with care, handling, and safety. But the committee also recognized that the choice would carry significant public relations implications because the mascot would symbolize the Academy. In the committee's view, the mascot should possess characteristics suggestive of the Air Force's primary mission—to fly and fight.

Always stately, the falcon commands a regal presence. Reprinted from the book *Fauconnerie: Catalogue Illustre.* Paris, 1890.

Choosing a Mascot

For this reason, the committee quickly eliminated domestic animals and turned its attention to birds of prey.

The eagle and the falcon were the principal birds discussed. In its research, the committee learned that many birds of prey are renowned for their rapid and powerful flight, made possible by a great wingspread. Furthermore, their tremendous speed and power, extraordinarily keen eyesight, and great ferocity are aided by strong, hooked beaks and sharp, curved talons that are formidable weapons in the pursuit of game. These characteristics eminently qualified birds of prey as hunters of the sky. The committee, therefore, concluded that birds of prey were the "most suitable candidates" for a mascot.

There were four reasons why the eagle was considered to be less desirable than the falcon. First, the eagle was the national symbol and should probably not be used by a lesser organization. Bald eagles and Golden eagles were also protected by the Bald Eagle Act. Second, in the strictest sense, some eagles subsisted "on carrion or game caught by, and stolen from other birds." Third, little was known about the training of eagles, whereas falconry was "an ancient and well-documented art with present day devotees." Finally, as the eagle was the national symbol, its capture or use was greatly restricted by game laws in many areas.

The committee noted that the falcon was the only wild creature that could be trained without being confined. Falconry, however, was "an arduous and time consuming task" and it might be very difficult to find qualified individuals to train the falcons. In addition, it would be necessary to have several birds on hand at all times as some losses would have to be anticipated. Nonetheless, the committee pointed out that since the falcon could be carried "on the fist" and not always have to be confined in a cage, it would present fewer problems in training than other undomesticated creatures. Moreover, the falcon with its piercing black eyes, noble carriage, and aggressive disposition, was considered to possess considerable personality and color.

Its deliberations concluded, the committee made the following recommendations:

1. That the Class of 1959 be asked to make a selection at some time prior to the end of their first year.
2. That the choice be limited to animals or birds possessing characteristics typifying the Air Force as a combat service.
3. That some type of falcon be adopted.

A hood is used to cover the head and the eyes of the falcon, keeping it calm. Courtesy Special Collections, Air Force Academy Library.

Dr. Harold M. Webster, a nationally known falconer, who was very helpful in getting the new Academy started in falconry, has provided the following interesting story about the cadets' choice of the falcon as their mascot:

> A front-page article appeared in the *Denver Post* featuring a story of how the cadets were in the process of picking a mascot to represent the Air Force Academy. The picture accompanying the article showed an old goshawk, *not* a falcon. I took it on myself to right this error. I already had almost twenty years in the sport of falconry at that time, and felt that it would not reflect well on a new service academy to begin under the shadow of a basic error. I telephoned the office of Superintendent Lt. Gen. H. R. Harmon and, after being shuttled around by three or four staff members, finally ended up with General Harmon himself. He asked if I would be so kind as to come to his office and that he would send a staff car to make it a bit easier. We had a long discussion and I advised him I had a new tiercel (male) Peale's peregrine that might bring a vote much sooner if only the Cadet Wing could see him fly. The general then asked if we could meet the next day, September 24, 1955, on the parade field at Lowry Air Force Base at 3:00 P.M.
>
> When I arrived at Lowry, the cadets were already in formation on the parade ground. I spoke briefly with the general; he wondered if there were any special procedures to follow. I advised him just to let the tiercel fly and take the pigeon; then the cadets could approach and watch the raptor feed. He told the cadets of those restrictions, and I then removed the hood from the tiercel and liberated him. He was about four months of age and was reasonably strong on the wing and began climbing. When he got to 4,000 feet I felt it was high enough as the day was temperate and I did not know what he might do if he got heated up. The pigeon was then liberated and started flying back toward the closest dormitory building only to be struck by the tiercel and killed almost instantly. The cadets set up a loud cheer announcing their approval, and I went to pick up the raptor. As soon as the bird was on my fist, the general asked if the cadets could come a bit closer. I nodded yes and he signaled an old infantry sign ... on the double, gather here. There was a rush and we were immediately surrounded by the cadets who wanted a closer look ... and they all seemed happy that the vote ... taken the very next day ... was almost unanimous in picking the falcon, although not any specific species or sex, as their choice of a mascot.

The Cadets Make Their Choice. On September 25, 1955, at their noon meal, the cadets of the Class of 1959 selected the falcon as their mascot. Five days later, Capt. Harrison H. D. Heiberg, Jr., was appointed the first officer-in-charge (OIC), or director, of the Academy's falconry program.

The Academy Acquires Its Falcons

When the members of the Cadet Wing selected the falcon as their mascot in September 1955, the Academy possessed no birds. The first were acquired through donations from enthusiasts of the sport of falconry and from others who also had an interest in seeing the Academy program succeed. In October 1955, Dr. Hal Webster again assisted the Academy by loaning his falcon so that it could be displayed "on the fist" in Denver University's stadium during the Academy's first football game. This was a Peale's peregrine falcon named **Captain Helene** that had been taken from an eyrie (nesting area) in British Columbia by Dr. Webster and Frank L. Beebe, another well-known falconer.

Dr. Webster also arranged for the capture of a tundra peregrine falcon on Assateague Island, Maryland, by William Turner of Washington, D. C. At the suggestion of Cadet Richard B. Goetze, the bird was named **Mach I** (the technical term for the speed of sound). **Mach I** was trained and first flown to the lure by Cadet Frederick E. Frey. While participating in the filming of *Wings of Tomorrow* in 1956, **Mach I** was lost. She was found dead west of Littleton, Colorado in 1960, having managed to survive four years in the wild.

Kris was the Academy's first gyrfalcon. This bird was a white-phase passage tiercel (a grown male) that had been captured in 1952 and given to the Academy in March 1956 by Colonel Meredith. **Kris** was not well and Colonel Meredith hoped that the Academy would be able to cure him. Unfortunately **Kris** died the day of General Harmon's retirement parade (July 27, 1956). The beautifully mounted bird is displayed in the office of the Director of Athletics.

Dr. Webster went to Alaska in 1956 and returned with two, gray-phase gyrfalcon fledglings. He gave one of them, **Kris II**, to the Academy. **Kris II** died accidentally in August 1956 when he fell off of his perch, hit a wall, and broke his neck.

Mach I, a peregrine falcon and the first Air Force Academy mascot, 1955–1956. Photo courtesy Special Collections, Air Force Academy Library.

Athol, a white-phase gyrfalcon, was taken from the wild with the permission of the Danish government by Dr. Webster at Point Athol, Greenland, in June 1960. **Athol** died in 1969, was mounted, and is displayed in the Academy Library.

Baffin was the next gyrfalcon to be acquired by the Academy. She was captured by Capt. Richard Graham on Baffin Island with the permission of the Canadian government and presented to the Cadet Wing in 1965. **Baffin** performed for the first time at a football game in November 1972 and flew out of the stadium, but was recaptured by Dr. Webster using a ladder from a Denver fire department truck. She died in 1978 after thirteen years as the "Queen of the Mews" and is mounted and on permanent display in Arnold Hall.

Soraya was a white-phase gyrfalcon received in January 1989 as a retired breeding falcon. At the age of seventeen, she was too old to fly and was used for educational display. She died in 1992 at the age of twenty.

Blizzard, also a white-phase gyrfalcon, hatched in 1975 and was given to the Academy in 1992 by a falconer who raised birds commercially. A retired breeder living out her retirement years, **Blizzard** died in 1994 at the age of nineteen, was mounted, and is displayed in the Department of Biology.

Glacier was a white-phase gyrfalcon captured for the Academy by Dr. James Enderson, a Colorado College professor, and Capt. Gerry Henningsen in July 1980, on the Seward Peninsula, Alaska. **Glacier** flew free for the last time on October 22, 1980, and flew away. He was recovered about an hour later and from then on flew only for exercise on a long line called a "creance." He was the Academy mascot for over fifteen years and died in 1995. He was also mounted and is on display in the Field House.

Aurora, a captive-bred, white-phase gyrfalcon, was hatched in the spring of 1996 and was five to six weeks old when purchased for the Falconry Club by the Academy's Association of Graduates. In Roman mythology, Aurora was the goddess of the dawn; her gyrfalcon namesake became the Academy's official mascot.

After **Mach I,** several other peregrine falcons were given to the Academy. **Houdini** was donated in 1970 by the Arizona-Sonora Desert Museum and was used in an early unsuccessful breeding effort. **Amanda** was given to the Academy by the U.S. Fish and Wildlife Service (USFWS) to be held as evidence in a trial. **Athena** and **Phoenix,** two anatum (along with Peale and tundra, the three subtypes of the North American peregrine falcon) peregrine sisters, were given to the Academy by the Colorado Division of Wildlife (DOW) in February 1994. They had been taken away from their previous owner and were both ill with bumblefoot—a disease caused primarily by unsanitary or incorrect perches and improper talon trimming. The Academy was expected to heal them and to allow them to molt out badly damaged feathers and then to use them for public relations and educational activities. The Falconry Club was very proud to be able to report that these birds were brought back to health and trained to fly to the lure in time to demonstrate them in the fall of

The Academy Acquires Its Falcons

1994. They were the first peregrine falcons to fly over football games in twenty years.

Many prairie falcons have been acquired by the Academy over the years and some have an interesting history. Although the Academy acquired its first prairie falcon in January 1956 (also a gift from Dr. Harold Webster), the original prairie falcon mascots were **Castor, Jezebel, Pollux,** and **Lucifer**. They were all taken as eyasses (chicks) from eyries along the Colorado Front Range in June 1956 by a party including Captain Heiberg, the Falconry Club's first OIC; John Flavin, a Denver ornithologist; Maj. Jack C. Young, an Academy staff legal officer; and Harold Webster. These birds had a spotty history. **Castor** died at the Academy in 1959, killed by another falcon. **Jezebel** was given to Dr. Robert M. Stabler, Professor of Zoology at Colorado College, an expert on the diseases of raptors and a great supporter of the Academy. **Pollux** was given to a private falconer who retrained him and released him to the wild in Canada. **Lucifer** was the most illustrious of these original mascots; she was the first falcon to fly free at a football game (Air Force versus Colorado School of Mines, October 20, 1956). Her handler was Cadet Kenneth S. Thom, Class of 1959.

The first falcon to perform at a night football game was **Hungry**, also a prairie falcon. Her performance over George Washington University's stadium was witnessed by President Eisenhower. One of **Hungry**'s tail feathers was taken to the moon on *Apollo* XV by Col. D. R. Scott. Reportedly, the prairie falcon **Nike** was

Cadet Kenneth S. Thom with *Lucifer*, 1956.
Photo by Capt. Harrison H. D. Heiberg, Jr.
Courtesy The Archives of American Falconry.

trained in 1960 by Maj. William L. Richardson, Jr., the second OIC and director of the falconry program, to "attack" the Army mule. **Jock**, a captive-bred falcon, was lost in Tokyo, Japan, while its handler was practicing for a performance during the Mirage Bowl in 1981. He was recovered and given to the Tama Zoo in Tokyo.

Milo was a prairie falcon captive-bred in 1985. He performed successfully during the football season that year but was killed during training the following January by a wild adult goshawk. He was mounted and is displayed at the Academy Visitors Center.

Bartles and **Jaymes** were prairie falcons taken from a Franktown, Colorado, eyrie in June 1987. Both were popular flyers. **Bartles** appeared on the national television show *Our House* in 1988. Both birds were placed in breeding

Cody, a prairie falcon and the Air Force Academy's best performing bird since 1992.
Photo courtesy Office of the Director of Falconry, Air Force Academy.

Falcon hoods range from the simple to the more elaborate, as shown to the right.
Courtesy Special Collections, Air Force Academy Library.

projects in late 1988. Ten months later **Bartles** was killed by his "mate." **Jaymes** was paired with **Darian** in 1988 and **Thunder** in 1992 but no fertile eggs were produced from either pair. **Jaymes** and **Thunder** were given to a rehabilitator in December 1994 and released to the wild the following spring.

Cody, a wild prairie falcon, was taken from an eyrie near Larkspur, Colorado, in June 1992. One of the best performers the Academy has ever produced, **Cody** completed his ninth flying season in 2001, the most ever by an Academy falcon.

Maximus, a male prairie falcon, was taken from a South Park, Colorado, eyrie in 2000; **Max** first flew at a football game at four months of age.

Several birds from other species of falcons have left their mark in the history of the falconry program. **Skip** was a merlin falcon given to the Academy by the Calgary Zoo in July 1984. He was a rehabilitated bird and was named after Lt. Gen. W. W. (Skip) Scott, Jr., then the Academy's Superintendent. He was the first merlin falcon to be displayed by the Academy.

Patrick was a kestrel falcon donated to the Academy by the Colorado DOW in 1982. **Patrick** was also an injured, rehabilitated bird and flew for cub scout pack and elementary school demonstrations. He flew away in April 1985.

Titanium, a tiercel Peale's peregrine, was traded to the Academy for a female anatum that was born at the Academy in 1999. **Titanium** was such a strong flyer a parachute was devised to slow him down. During performances, when **Titanium** grabbed the lure a drag chute deployed to keep him in the stadium.

These accounts illustrate the lives and performances of some of the falcons handled by the Academy Falconry Club over the years and give some idea of the successes and failures inevitably experienced

in a program that deals with wild creatures. The cadets often became quite attached to their birds during their years of close association and the exhilaration and pride they felt from successful performances by their falcons made all the patience required and time spent with their charges worthwhile.

Secretary of the Air Force Dudley C. Sharp, with Air Force Academy Superintendent Maj. Gen. William S. Stone, presents two falcons, gifts of the King of Saudi Arabia, to Cadets R. W. Arnold, D. P. Wood, and R. K. Johnson, June 8, 1960. Photo courtesy Office of the Director of Falconry, Air Force Academy.

Assistance from Individuals and Groups

The ultimate objective of the Academy falconry program, of course, was to show the mascot as favorably as possible, preferably in free flight. To do so required a sophisticated operation developed from scratch. This was not achieved without problems and disappointments. Most were the result of lack of experience. Without the extraordinary support of a number of individuals and organizations with special expertise the venture would probably have been abandoned.

Among the individuals especially helpful in getting the Academy's program started were: Capt. Harrison H. D. Heiberg, Jr., the first officer-in-charge of the Academy's falconry program; Col. Russell L. Meredith, USAF, the President of the Falconry Club of America in 1955; Dr. Harold M. Webster, Jr., a well-known Denver falconer and author; John Flavin, a

The first falcon mascots were delivered to Stapleton Field, Denver, October 6, 1955. Captain Harrison Heiberg accepts the carefully packaged falcons from an airline stewardess. Photo courtesy Special Collections, Air Force Academy Library.

Col. (Dr.) Lawrence E. Schaad, Director of the Air Force Academy falconry program from 1981 to 1995.
Photo courtesy Colonel Schaad.

Lt. Col. S. Kent Carnie, USA (Ret.), Curator of The Archives of American Falconry. Carnie is carrying a hybrid falcon—a gyrfalcon and peregrine.
Photo by J. Kidmore. Courtesy The Archives of American Falconry.

Denver ornithologist; Col. (Dr.) James C. McIntyre, who, as one of the early OICs of the program, pioneered falcon breeding at the Academy; Professor James H. Enderson of Colorado College, the Academy program consultant from 1977 until 2000; William S. Dollar, an Academy program consultant since 1984 and an expert in the breeding of falcons; John Karger of Last Chance Forever of San Antonio, Texas, who retrained over twenty of the Academy's older birds to hunt and released them into the wild; Lt. Col. S. Kent Carnie, USA, (Ret.) Curator, Archives of American Falconry; Dr. Robert M. Stabler, Professor of Zoology at Colorado College and a master falconer; and Maj. Jack C. Young of the Academy Legal Office in 1956, an enthusiastic falconer who assisted the Academy's program in many ways. Other key program participants over the years were Frank L. Beebe, co-author with Dr. Harold M. Webster of *North American Falconry and Hunting Hawks*, and donor to the Academy of a Peale's peregrine falcon in 1955; Capt. William H. Halliwell of Dr. McIntyre's staff who did much of the early work in the treatment and rehabilitation of raptors at the Academy; Col. (Dr.) Lawrence E. Schaad, OIC of the Academy program for fourteen years (1981–1995); Walter Crawford, the head of the Raptor Rehabilitation and Propagation Project who, along with others, gave the Academy a captively-raised Richardson's merlin falcon; and Dan L. Cecchine, Jr., a Colorado Springs area falconer who donated two, captive-bred tiercel peregrines.

Thus, right from the start and throughout the history of its program, the Academy had the encouragement, advice, and support of national and local leaders and experts in the art of falconry.

Several organizations have also been crucial to the success of the falconry program. Foremost among them are the regulatory agencies, the U.S. Fish and Wildlife Service (USFWS), and the Colorado Department of Wildlife (DOW).

Some years ago the peregrine falcon faced extinction due to the widespread use of the pesticide DDT and its introduction into the falcons' food chain. This caused falcon eggs to be too thin to withstand the brooding process. As a result, peregrines were declared an endangered species and were nationally protected. The USFWS and the Colorado DOW strictly control the hunting or taking of all falcons from the wild, maintaining them in captivity, and breeding or transferring them. Accordingly, cadet falconers and their OICs are required to pass licensing tests to possess, train, breed, or transfer falcons. Licenses must be renewed every two years and annual reports are submitted covering the activities of the program.

The Academy has maintained excellent rapport with these two agencies and, from time to time, has been granted waivers to regulations in order to take a few fledglings from the wild when the breeding program failed to produce birds in sufficient numbers to sustain the flying demonstrations. The Academy worked especially closely with the DOW during the years Colonel (Dr.) McIntyre directed the falconry program. Dr. McIntyre, a pioneer in the veterinary treatment of birds of prey, enjoyed a national reputation as a rehabilitator and a designer of treatment regimens and protocols. During his tenure great strides were made in these aspects of what was then a very new science, and the Academy worked with the Colorado DOW and the USFWS to house injured birds for rehabilitation or for use as evidence in court cases. Today many

Col. (Dr.) James C. McIntyre, Director of Falconry from 1965 to 1975. Photo courtesy Office of the Director of Falconry, Air Force Academy.

schools of veterinary medicine have such programs and rehabilitators are common in many areas. For this reason the Academy is no longer involved in the rehabilitation of injured birds, although it continues to be interested in advancements in the veterinary and nutritional fields.

Birds excess to the needs of the Academy, with the approval of the Colorado DOW, have been given to a number of organizations including the Cheyenne Mountain Zoo in Colorado Springs; the Colorado Aspen Center for Environmental Studies; the Raptor Rehabilitation and Propagation Project, Saint Louis, Missouri; the Last Chance Forever Organization, San Antonio, Texas (given over twenty birds); and the Birds of Prey Rehabilitation Foundation, Broomfield, Colorado. The U.S. Air Force's Bird Strike Program at Nellis Air Force Base in Nevada received falcons

William "Sam" Dollar. Skilled falconer and consultant to the Air Force Academy falconry program since 1984. Photo courtesy W. S. Dollar.

Professor James H. Enderson, Colorado College, Colorado Springs, Colo. Expert falconer and consultant to the Air Force Academy falconry program from 1977 to 2000. Photo courtesy James H. Enderson.

from the Academy as an experiment to frighten other birds away from the runways.

The Peregrine Fund of Boise, Idaho (until 1984 located at Fort Collins, Colorado) has been a special friend of the Academy falconry program for many years. Until the fall of 1983 when the Academy began its own falcon feeding program, the Fund had regularly provided the coturnix quail used to feed the Academy's falcons. In 1980 when the Academy was experiencing problems breeding falcons, the Fund provided the Academy with three prairie falcons to train for demonstrations. At other times the Fund used young Academy birds as foster babies for its young peregrine parents to stimulate their parenting instincts. Then after about three weeks of brooding, the babies were returned to the Academy for their real parents to finish raising. This cooperative relationship resulted in a stronger and more successful Academy program. The Peregrine Fund has bred and released peregrine falcons to the wild throughout the West. These efforts played a major role in the removal of the anatum peregrine from the Federal Endangered Species List in August 1999.

Facilities and Equipment

Early in the history of falconry it was learned that to enjoy the sport and the prestige that possession of these birds offered, an extensive establishment was required. It is no wonder that this activity with its extensive facilities came to be referred to as the sport of kings! The place where the birds are sheltered, fed, trained, nourished, and bred is called a "mews."

In April 1956, Capt. Harrison H. D. Heiberg, Jr., the OIC of the fledgling falconry program at the Air Force Academy's temporary site in Denver, asked Maj. Jack C. Young, an experienced falconer serving in the Academy's legal office, for his opinion relative to the requirements for a falcon mews at the permanent Academy site in Colorado Springs, then under construction. Young specified that the following were needed to meet the minimum requirements:

Space. The mews should provide two types of space for the birds—an open area in which they could be weathered on the block (their personal perch) and a closed

The classroom at the mews.
Photo by MSgt. Kenneth L. Carter. Courtesy Office of the Director of Falconry, Air Force Academy.

and protected area in which they could be shielded from the elements. The open area should allow exposure to the morning and afternoon sun and the closed area should offer protection from the noonday sun, precipitation, and drafts. In each instance the space provided for each bird should be sufficient to allow freedom of movement on the leash with a minimum radius of three feet.

Water. The mews should contain at least one water outlet because the amount of water needed for the proper daily care of the birds would be substantial. In addition to a daily bath for each bird, the blocks or perches would require frequent washing and the grass-covered "weathering" area daily watering.

Electricity. The mews should contain sufficient electrical outlets to provide adequate lighting for handling the birds during hours of darkness. This handling would include the routine care of the birds following football games or other events, the manning (calming) and gentling of new birds, the treatment of sick birds, and the use of lights to facilitate the molt (yearly shedding of old and regrowth of new feathers). In addition, electricity would be needed for a small refrigerator unit to store fresh food for the birds.

Storage or work room. The mews should contain sufficient storage and work room for equipment such as blocks, screened perches, bath pans, scales, hoods, jesses (leather restraining straps), leashes, swivels, brooms, mops, falconer bags, gauntlets, and other items. In addition the storage room should be able to accommodate a work table, meat block, refrigerator unit, water outlet, and wash basin. There should also be a large and permanent screened perch that would suffice for up to three sick or injured birds.

Food storage. The mews should have proper food storage facilities. Since falcons eat only fresh meat and economy requires the purchase of meat in relatively large quantities, a refrigerator unit is the normal solution. Food for human consumption, however, should not be stored in the same refrigerator as the bulk of the meat purchased for the falcons is not inspected.

Drainage. The mews should be well drained. Many falcon diseases and various parasites affecting the birds are directly attributable to damp, poorly drained mews. The health of the birds as well as their appearance depend primarily upon their being provided a dry, well-drained, well-ventilated, clean living area.

Security. The mews should offer complete security from molestation by predatory wild animals and birds as well as house pets that may be loose in the area. In this connection the great horned owls, goshawks, and eagles, all of which are found in the area of the permanent Academy site, are the natural enemies of the falcon. Needless to say, a falcon tied to a block is almost defenseless against these birds and against dogs, feral cats, or coyotes. In addition, the security of the mews should include protection against molestation or theft. The relatively delicate and high-strung temperament of falcons also precludes their being handled by anyone not initiated in the art. Security of the mews, therefore, is an absolute necessity.

Facilities and Equipment

In sum, the permanent mews at the Air Force Academy should, at a minimum, meet the above requirements and in addition should present an attractive appearance in harmony with other construction at the permanent Academy site. The construction of an adequate and well-planned mews would greatly facilitate the health and welfare of the birds and would allow a minimum expenditure of time and effort on the part of the cadets responsible for their care and training.

According to Major Young, the Air Force Academy had already made great strides in arousing public interest in and admiration for the falcons and this attention also reflected positively on the Academy. Game conservationists had long sought to promote this type of public education and viewed the Academy's activities favorably. Although the prairie falcon was a protected bird in Colorado, the state Department of Wildlife not only voiced no objections but offered to assist the Academy's program. Because the falcons would be observed almost daily by the general public and representatives of numerous organizations of all types, it was imperative that the care, maintenance, and housing of the birds be above reproach. A proper mews would help achieve this goal.

The Academy Acquires Its Mews. Major Young's recommendations became a blueprint for the future Academy mews, but its construction and smooth operation were achieved only gradually over many years. Initially, falcons at Lowry Air Force Base in Denver, temporary site of the Air Force Academy, were kept in an improvised mews. When the Cadet Wing moved to the permanent facilities north of Colorado Springs in 1958, falcons were kept in a cage under Vandenberg Hall. In 1960, the first mews was built just north of the main cadet area. This building, housing the falcons and falconry program supplies and equipment, was a two-sided, 12 x 12 foot cinder block structure with an outdoor weathering area where birds could be blocked (placed on individual perches). Later, a new mews building and, by 1973, two additional buildings were added to the falconry enclave. The facility was named the McIntyre Mews on August 8, 1979, in memory of Colonel McIntyre, OIC from

The weathering pen at the mews.
Photo by MSgt. Kenneth L. Carter. Courtesy Office of the Director of Falconry, Air Force Academy.

July 1965 to December 1975. (Colonel McIntyre died October 24, 1976.) In January 1988, two more buildings were completed. These prefabricated concrete structures located at the north edge of the mews compound provided a quail incubating area, a classroom, and storage. The fine facilities now available to support the falconry program at the Academy took over thirty years to acquire and are the result of much effort and assistance from skilled individuals and devoted friends.

The first falcon mews, Lowry Air Force Base, Colorado, 1957. Photo by Capt. Harrison H.D. Heiberg, Jr. Courtesy The Archives of American Falconry.

The main office of the mews. Photo courtesy Office of the Director of Falconry, Air Force Academy.

Breeding Falcons in Captivity

Captive breeding of raptors in North America was not attempted until 1964; at that time there was only one successful raptor breeding program in the world. That year Dr. Webster's and Frank Beebe's extremely important *North American Falconry and Hunting Hawks* was published. It set forth the details of how to capture and train raptors. The book ignited widespread enthusiasm in falconry, stimulating captive-breeding programs. Not long after he became OIC of the Academy's falconry program in 1965, Colonel McIntyre began to study the feasibility of a breeding project to produce the Academy's own birds.

Since older falcons molt (shed their feathers) between April and September every year after their first year, it was at first considered to be too difficult to use older birds for flying demonstrations during the football season in late summer and early fall. This is the reason why success in the breeding program was so important. It takes ten to twelve weeks to train a new bird to fly well before a crowd in a football stadium. The birds hatch in May so the cadets had to train them in time to have them flying in a stadium by late August.

Starting in 1995, the program focus was changed from bringing new falcons into training each year to maintaining the proven performers. Prior to this time, up to six new falcons were required annually to provide flyers for the academic year. With this change in practice, only one or two new falcons were required and the cadets were able to train and fly more seasoned performers.

Until 1965, the OICs of the falconry program, all with a strong interest in and devotion to the sport, came from a variety of military backgrounds. Since 1965 (beginning with Colonel McIntyre), a veterinarian has served as the OIC, providing expertise in preventive medicine, avian husbandry, and animal behavior (although perhaps without as strong a background in falconry). In 1977, the program was further strengthened by the

The breeding pen at the mews. Photo by MSgt. Kenneth L. Carter. Courtesy Special Collections, Air Force Academy Library.

addition of a civilian consultant, Dr. James H. Enderson, a nationally known falconer, a captive breeder of falcons, and Professor and Head of the Department of Biology at Colorado College. Through his advice, contacts, and extensive experience, Dr. Enderson greatly aided the captive-breeding and training programs.

Breeding Efforts Begin. In 1971 the Academy tried to breed two peregrine falcons. One, named **Houdini,** was given to the Academy by the Arizona-Sonora Desert Museum in Tucson, Arizona; the other, named **Belle,** was a gift from a private donor. This effort continued until 1973 but was unsuccessful. In 1974, however, four young prairie falcons hatched from the captive-breeding program. From then on the falconry program concentrated its efforts on raising prairie falcons.

Captive Breeding Flourishes. Since 1974 the Academy falconry program has had a successful captive-breeding program, producing at least sixty prairie falcons with an average of four chicks per year from 1976 through 1986. In 1980, only one chick hatched and the Peregrine Fund gave the Academy three eyasses hatched by the Fund. In 1986, only two chicks hatched from the Academy and two chicks were taken from the wild. These were used as flyers and then were paired as breeders to improve blood lines in the breeders. Overall, however, the program was so successful that between 1976 and 1986, the Academy gave away forty-three captively raised prairie falcons (over 70 percent of the birds that hatched) after they became excess to needs. They were given to zoos, wildlife parks, captive-breeding projects, bird air strike programs, and to groups that trained them to hunt and then released them into the wild. After some years of taking birds from the wild the Academy was now in a position to return birds to their natural environment.

Sometimes There Were Problems. The period from 1986 to 1994 was a difficult time for the Academy breeding program. One eyass was killed during capture and not enough birds were hatched to sustain the demonstration program. In fact, from 1987 through 1994, the breeding project produced no young even though new pairs were established and many changes were made to the breeding chambers. In four instances, through unlucky pairing of breeding pairs, male birds were killed by their mates.

From 1974 until 1986, there had been two pairs of breeders. Because of anticipated breeding problems, a third pair was started in 1986. That pair was broken up in 1987 and another pair begun that August. Unfortunately the female immediately killed its mate. The next year the Academy

The falcon mascot is a popular symbol as reflected by its use in the Academy's 557th Flying Training Squadron patch. Courtesy Special Collections, Air Force Academy Library.

gave away one of the older pairs and tried to start another two pairs. In both instances, the female killed the male. The only remaining pair continued, but had to be separated when the female showed aggression toward the male. From 1990 through 1993 the program had only two pairs of breeders, neither of which was successful. In 1994 there were three pairs of breeders; however, only two produced eggs and none were fertile.

Beginning in 1986 the Colorado DOW again allowed the Academy to take birds from the wild. They included young prairies from Eagles' Peak, a cliff directly west of the Academy Visitors Center where the DOW had previously released peregrines.

Recovery. Taking advantage of the lessons learned from the loss of the breeding birds, a number of improvements were made in the program to insure compatibility of the birds paired together. These efforts finally paid off. In 1995, there were again three pairs of breeders. All were successful with eight of sixteen eggs fertile, producing four young hatching in May and four in June 1995.

From 1996 to 1998 the prairie falcons in the breeding program did not produce any fertile eggs that resulted in successful hatches. In 1999 the oldest pair of prairie breeders was donated to the Cheyenne Mountain Zoo and a new pair of peregrine falcons was introduced into the breeding program. **Phoenix,** the female, was donated to the Academy by the Colorado DOW and **Havoc,** the male, was donated to the program by Sam Dollar, a local falconer. Both of these birds had already been handled extensively at the Academy. **Havoc**

A lapel pin celebrates the F-16 aircraft, also nicknamed the *Fighting Falcon*. Courtesy Special Collections, Air Force Academy Library.

had been trained to fly at Academy parades and **Phoenix** had traveled to numerous educational and recruiting events throughout the nation with cadet handlers and public affairs officials. **Phoenix** and **Havoc** produced two fertile eggs in their first season together. Two chicks hatched and one survived, a female. This was the first peregrine successfully hatched at the Academy.

Despite the problems encountered, the Academy's initiative in establishing a captive-breeding program has provided a successful example and valuable shared experience for falconry throughout North America.

Breeding Facilities. Each breeding chamber has a ledge or box containing gravel for the birds to use as a nest or scrape. Astroturf-covered perches provide the birds perching space. Pen dimensions are approximately 8 x 14, 8 x 12, and 8 x 10 feet (all originally with an 8 foot ceiling). In 1990, Colonel Schaad, the OIC, modified two of the breeding chambers to raise the ceiling. The next year Academy civil engineers installed skylights in each of the two enlarged chambers. The two larger pens, each with a nest ledge, have been used successfully to fledge young falcons. (During fledging, the birds grow all their

Baby peregrine eyasses photographed in Canada in the wild.
Photo by Arvy F. Kysely. Courtesy Special Collections, Air Force Academy Library.

feathers, learn to fly, and gain their independence.) The third and smaller pen was built in the fall of 1984. All have windows allowing light to enter.

No artificial heating or lighting is available to the breeder birds. They are fed once a day and that is enough to keep them "fed up" (fat). Falcon females lay an egg every other day until a clutch of four to six eggs is down. The birds begin incubating eggs (both male and female sit on the eggs) about the time the last egg is laid. The parents are allowed to sit on the eggs about a week, providing natural incubation. The eggs are then candled (placed in front of a high intensity light in a darkened room to make the silhouette of an embryo visible). Fertile eggs are returned to the parents to complete incubation. Infertile eggs are removed, blown out, and saved for educational use. If eggs are pulled early in the incubation, the female will begin a new clutch (i.e., double clutching) almost two weeks to the day the eggs are removed. This often provides not only more eggs, but fertile eggs when the first eggs are infertile. Parents will incubate the eggs for the normal incubation period of thirty-four days although they may remain on eggs much longer (as long as two weeks to eighteen days past hatching date).

At one time, eggs were purposely double clutched to provide young chicks that could be used as foster babies for young peregrine parents at the Peregrine Fund, which would incubate the eggs artificially. The Fund would use the recently hatched chicks as foster babies for two to three weeks and then return them to the Academy. With the Peregrine Fund's relocation to Boise, Idaho, it became very difficult to transport incubating eggs and brooding chicks. The last year the Academy assisted the Peregrine Fund in that aspect of the cooperative agreement was 1985.

Raising Falcons to Maturity. To prevent imprinting, or the association of a young chick with a human that can result in screaming and other bad behaviors, the young falcons are left with their parents until they are "hard penned" (feathers have grown out completely or are not still "in the blood" or growing). When feathers are hard penned, they are much stronger and more resistant to breakage. Birds are usually not hard penned until they are eight weeks of age.

Feeding the Falcons

In the early days of the Academy program, birds were fed chicken necks, beef hearts, and venison—food that almost all falconers were using in the early 1960s. Sometime during his tenure from 1965 to 1975, Colonel McIntyre arranged a donation from the DeKalb Hatchery of Hudson, Colorado, of day-old cockrel (male chicken) chicks that were being hatched in an egg-layer production operation. This donation continued every year, a thousand chicks in the fall and two thousand in the spring, until the mid 1980s. From 1983 to 1985, the Academy needed only the two batches of 1,000 chicks each spring.

In early 1983 the Academy received from the Peregrine Fund, then located in Fort Collins, Colorado, several hundred frozen quail. These were needed to feed the breeder falcons. That fall, in anticipation of its imminent move to Boise, Idaho, the Peregrine Fund gave the Academy live coturnix quail, which began a new era in food production for the Academy program.

Beginning in the summer of 1984 the Academy began raising its own quail. This program was continued until 2000 when it then became possible to obtain processed frozen quail commercially. Normal production from 1985 was about 100 eggs per day with about 200 eggs set in one of four Roll-X incubators every four days. Once eggs began hatching, they were transferred to an old, wooden still-air incubator. An approximately 75 percent hatch was often obtained, with 65 percent being the average. This was comparable to the 65 percent experienced by the Peregrine Fund, a rate of quail production sufficient for the Academy's program. Quail chicks were brooded a few days and then transferred to larger pens to be raised until they began laying eggs (about five to six weeks). At this point the quail were humanely killed and then fed to the falcons. Several hundred were maintained in a freezer as a backup food source should the quail production rate fall.

In January 1988 Buildings 2184 and 2185, both prefabricated concrete, were constructed. Building 2184 has a small classroom and quail hatching laboratory plus an unheated storage area. Building 2185, with weathering pen attached, was the quail raising facility. It also has an external mat washrack attached. Since 1988, from these two buildings, the program raised 4,000–8,000 quail per year—enough to feed the Academy's falcons and to provide most of the coturnix quail used as food for peregrine releases in Colorado during 1988–1990.

Contributions to the Art and Science of Falconry

Innovations in Medical Care. During Colonel McIntyre's tenure as OIC of the falconry program from 1965 to 1975, the Air Force Academy accomplished much in the area of raptor rehabilitation. Along with some work in nutrition, Dr. McIntyre pioneered in injury repair and medical treatment. About the time that he retired, wildlife laws became more strict resulting in the reduction of injuries to wild raptors. Consequently, from 1975 on, the Air Force Academy was not nearly as involved with rehabilitation efforts.

Preventive Medicine. Throughout the years, but especially since 1965 when veterinarians began to direct the falconry program, preventive medicine versus primary treatment has been heavily stressed. Although primary treatment is provided as needed, proper husbandry, nutrition, and talon and beak care (coping or trimming of the talons and beak) have been given special attention.

Captive Breeding. As far as is known, captive breeding of birds of prey was not attempted in the United States until about 1960 and was a relatively new science worldwide. When Dr. McIntyre arrived at the Academy as the Command Veterinarian, he volunteered to direct the falconry program and promptly began studying the possibilities of initiating captive breeding of falcons. His first efforts with peregrines in 1971 and 1972 failed, but in 1974 he successfully bred prairie falcons. Since then the Academy has continued developing effective breeding techniques and procedures and has actively shared its experience with other agencies.

As a Bird Repository. The Academy has established an excellent reputation for its care of birds and in recent years has been asked to keep injured or abused birds to be used as evidence in trials for the USFWS, and has kept young eyass birds, kestrels primarily, who needed another month or so before they were fully fledged. Additionally, beginning in 1987, the Academy accepted the responsibility to act as a repository for old breeder peregrines, gyrfalcons, and even merlins that, although no longer breeders, could be used in public education. **Phoenix,** an anatum peregrine from a 1973 hatch, arrived in August 1987 and lived until 1993. An anatum peregrine, **Lil,** hatched in 1976, came in August 1988. Both were from the Peregrine Fund. **Phoenix** lived for twenty and **Lil**

for twenty-one years. Old gyrfalcons **Soraya** and **Blizzard** were used until they died at the ages of nineteen (1988) and twenty (1992) respectively. An old merlin, **Sara** (hatched in 1981) arrived from falcon breeders in Corvallis, Oregon in February 1993.

Reprinted from *Fauconnerie: Catalogue Illustre.* Paris, 1890.

THE CADETS AND THEIR FALCONS

Organization of the Falconry Program

In 1955 the falconry program was a unique and unprecedented function peculiar to the new Air Force Academy. There were no prototype activities in the older service academies that would show the way. In fact there were no similar programs anywhere to help the program get started. Every action taken broke new ground and much of the progress obtained in the early years was based on trial and error.

Having selected a mascot and established a makeshift mews at Lowry Air Force Base, the Academy's temporary location, the next task was to create an organization that would provide for the welfare of the birds and stimulate cadet involvement. Then the falcon mascot could be displayed effectively and, it was hoped, trained to perform in a way that would meet the needs of organizational spirit and reflect credit on the Academy.

Initial Organization. The falconry program was initially organized as an athletic squad supervised by the Director of Athletics and oriented toward providing displays of the falcons in connection with athletic events. On March 11, 1957, Capt. Harrison H. D. Heiberg, Jr., the first OIC of the falconry program, established an official status for the volunteer "cadet falcon handlers" as they had come to be called. The Air Force Academy Athletic Association had assumed nominal ownership of the falcons in order to provide insurance coverage and had agreed to provide the financial support necessary for their maintenance. The cadet falcon handlers had up to this time not enjoyed athletic status except on days of athletic events. Captain Heiberg recommended that these cadets be reassigned from the Department of Athletics and be organized as an official cadet activity under the Commandant of Cadets.

After considerable discussion, the Commandant agreed. Thereupon, the cadet falcon handlers were dropped from the athletic squad lists and organized as a club, one of several official cadet appropriated fund activities under the Commandant's office. The club was provided an officer-in-charge (OIC), an assistant OIC, and a cadet of the first class as cadet-in-charge (CIC). The Air Force Academy Athletic Association was thus relieved of the responsibility to maintain the birds; the falcons henceforth would be supported by the cadet activities fund. The OIC was authorized to provide falcons and falcon handlers to display the birds or to conduct demonstrations at any athletic event at the request of the Director of Athletics.

Falconry Club, 1982–1983. Back row, left to right: Capt. Richard Postlewaite, Cadets Mike Finley, Mark Vanderburgh (with *Glacier*), John Zazworsky, Mark Abbott, Mark Deluca, Lt. Col. Larry Schaad. Front row: Cadets Betsy Vanderburgh, Brian Rath, Pat Smith, Arnold Gaus, Chuck Burnett, Peter Lewis. Photo courtesy Office of the Director of Falconry, Air Force Academy.

Falconry Club Operation. The responsibilities associated with the falconry program are shared by the OIC, the Assistant OIC, and the cadets. The administrative work, including the extensive interaction and reporting associated with the U.S. Fish and Wildlife Service and the Colorado Department of Wildlife (DOW), is handled by the OIC. Because falcons have been on the national list of protected species for many years, these authorities exercise strict control over their possession, handling, and transfer. The OIC and assistant OIC also handle supply matters, supervise the care and maintenance of the mews, organize appearances at away football games, and are in charge of the public relations scheduling. The cadets are responsible for the care and training of the falcons, their display and demonstrations, the training of new falcon handlers, and for the cleanliness of the mews.

Leadership Training. The falconry program is an excellent leadership laboratory. The first class cadets (seniors) have demanding supervisory and training responsibilities within the program and all the cadets find themselves constantly before the public as representatives of the Academy. At the end of each school year, one of the second class (junior) cadet handlers (there are usually four) is selected by the outgoing seniors to be the new CIC for the coming academic year. Each of the new first class cadets becomes chief of one of the four teams selected for the upcoming academic year. The ideal team is composed of a first class cadet, a second class cadet, and a third class cadet (sophomore). Each of the four teams is expected to train one of the performing falcons in time for the coming fall athletic season and will be responsible to care for one or more static (nonperforming) birds.

Selection of New Members. From the beginning of the spring semester until spring break, fourth class cadets (freshmen) who aspire to be cadet falconers learn about the mascot program, handle the prairie falcons under direct supervision of upper class cadet falconers, and do whatever else needs to be done to support the program. They work with the mascot program on available free afternoons at their own choosing. They log in the time that they spend at the mews and the tasks they have completed. There is no hard and fast amount of participation necessary to be selected a cadet falconer, but all candidates must demonstrate their interest while not neglecting their academic and military responsibilities. From as many as forty to fifty prospective falconers, attrition brings the number down to five to ten by the end of spring break.

From among those fourth class cadets who have been participating regularly during the apprentice period, four will be selected to represent their class for the rest of the time they are at the Academy. They will be evaluated for club membership by the upper class cadets based on three key areas: how well they work with the birds, how well they communicate with the public, and how well they get along with club members.

Before a cadet actually becomes a cadet falconer, he or she must successfully pass a raptor licensing examination administered by the Colorado DOW. The actual licensing test scores are not weighed in the falconry program selection process: it is considered a pass/fail event. The upper class cadet falconers are only told by the OIC which prospects received a passing score. Those who did not pass are removed from the selection process. Additional factors that play into the decision are the prospect's academic and athletic standing. Those cadets on any kind of probation are not likely to be chosen because the considerable time required to participate in the falconry program could further jeopardize their situation. The team must have cadets in good standing who can travel. The club seeks to maintain a strength of twelve cadets but attrition occasionally reduces the number to ten. It is made very clear to prospective cadet

Cadet Wendy Girton (member of the Class of 1982 and the first female cadet falcon handler). Photo courtesy Wendy Girton Corbett.

falconers that once selected, they are expected to be falconers for the remaining three years.

As a result of the fine reputation that cadet falconers have established, United Airlines permits cadet falconers to carry their birds on board on the fist when they travel to and from performances at games and other events. This is an important convenience and greatly appreciated and used regularly by the cadet handlers.

Group of cadet falconers from the classes of 1961, 1962, and 1963. Photo courtesy Office of the Director of Falconry, Air Force Academy.

Falcon Handler Training

Soon after the falcon was selected as the Academy's mascot, the idea of training the birds to perform, rather than merely showing them as static displays, captured the enthusiasm of the Cadet Wing; it soon became clear that this would be the main effort of the new program. In the middle of October 1955, cadets started to learn how to handle the falcons. The first cadet handler was Frederick E. Frey, a member of the Class of 1959. He was joined by three other handlers shortly afterward. Cadet Frey was the first cadet to fly **Mach I** to a lure (February 21, 1956). Since she was an immature bird when caught (called a passage bird), **Mach I** knew how to hunt and the risk of losing her was too great to use her in free flight in the stadium. The first bird to perform at a football game was **Lucifer,** handled by Cadet Kenneth S. Thom on October 20, 1956.

Since 1958 the birds have been routinely displayed at football and basketball games, hockey matches, and other sports events. They are normally flown at all home and most away football games and most cadet parades. The birds are also displayed at various air shows and other activities throughout the country and appear extensively in school presentations and at other educational venues.

The falconry program is an extremely time-consuming activity. The OIC averages about 100 hours per month working directly in support of the mascot program, and the cadets, already tightly scheduled, also contribute a tremendous amount of time to this year-round activity. In fact the falconry program demands as much time as would be required to participate in a varsity sport. During the academic year, just as in collegiate athletic programs, cadet falconers are "on-season" for two of the three seasons—fall, winter, and spring. In all three summer periods cadet falconers spend time training falcons to perform during the coming year.

Every fall, as needed, young prairie falcons are trained as performing mascots. These birds do not molt their first year. Molting occurs every year after the falcon's first year during April to September. During this time all birds of

Bells, when attached to the leg of the falcon, are used to locate the bird. The swivel device connects the leather jesses around a falcon's leg with a leash or creance line, and keeps it from getting tangled. Courtesy Special Collections, Air Force Academy Library.

A group of cadet falconers, "on-season" in fall of 2002, training their falcons. From left to right: Cadet First Class Ashley Watson, Cadet Third Class Chris Finkenstadt, Cadet Third Class Anthony Cannone (with a kestrel falcon), Cadet Third Class Krysta Peltzer, Lt. Col. Steve Niehoff, Director of Falconry, Cadet Third Class Dennis Muller (with a peregrine falcon), Cadet Second Class Joe Fixemer, Cadet Third Class Kim Herd (with a prairie falcon), Cadet Second Class Tyler Young, and Cadet Second Class Mike Heddinger. Photo courtesy Office of the Director of Falconry, Air Force Academy.

prey are stressed, fly with some difficulty, and tend to damage their new feathers if they are too active before the end of their molt. It has been found, however, that some birds complete their molt early and are good performers during the full football season, year after year.

All cadet falconers are on-season during the fall. This period extends from early August until the end of the football season. The falcon handlers normally spend from about 4:00 pm to 6:30 pm daily at the mews until all tasks have been completed. These include giving each flying mascot its daily flight training and its food ration at the end of the training sessions.

This daily training of the performing birds starts in the main cadet area where the birds begin to be conditioned to crowds and noise. By the time football season begins, the training has progressed to the football stadium. Routine flying training is conducted six days a week. On the seventh day the birds are fed but not flown. Cleaning and minor maintenance of facilities and equipment is primarily accomplished on Saturday mornings. Those cadets not traveling to an away football game must, on those occasions, take care of all the chores. The Falconry Club's OIC and assistant OIC do the weekday morning guard and falconry chores because the cadets are not normally free those hours during the academic year.

The winter season extends from the end of football season until President's Weekend in February. During this period only half of the cadet falconers are "on-season." The flying mascots have now finished their demonstrations in the

The distinctive falconry shoulder patch issued by the Commandant of Cadets and worn by newly selected cadet falconers.
Photo courtesy Office of the Director of Falconry, Air Force Academy.

The white falcon patch presented to cadet falconers by the Athletic Department following completion of their third class year.
Photo courtesy Office of the Director of Falconry, Air Force Academy.

The Air Force Academy minor letter monogram worn by cadet falconers. Photo courtesy Office of the Director of Falconry, Air Force Academy.

stadium and the OIC will have arranged to give away all but the best two or three flyers. After Christmas the effort is less on training the birds, and more on training the less experienced cadet falconers in flying the birds free to the lure.

This process continues until the birds begin to molt in mid-April. By this time, hopefully, prairie falcon eyasses have hatched. The chores must still be done and the mews is opened to tours, which will average three to four a week later in the spring.

The spring season extends from President's Weekend until graduation. Cadets on-season at this time include those who were not on-season during the winter. Tour groups visit the mews almost every day and are briefed and escorted through the facilities. The birds are still being flown until they begin their molt, and prospective cadet falconers are rapidly gaining experience and are competing for selection as new cadet falconers; these selections will be made by mid-May. Breeder falcons by now have laid eggs and some have hatched by the end of April or early May.

The summer at the Air Force Academy is divided into three, three-week-long periods. During each, some of the cadet falconers who have already had at least one year's experience, together with at least one new team member, volunteer to do "Mews Watch." This involves training the birds recently hatched to be flyers for the coming fall sports season. It takes at least six weeks of six- to eight-hour days working with a bird for it to be flying free. During the summer, cadets also make themselves available for public relations or educational events, sometimes up to six presentations a day, as well as accomplishing any projects or chores involving the birds and the mews. Both the new CIC of the Falconry Club and the OIC encourage cadets to do "Mews Watch" at least once. It is an invaluable experience as it gives cadet falconers much broader familiarity with the overall Academy falconry program. When all the cadet falconers return for the start of the fall semester, the organized teams composed of cadets of the upper three classes carry on with the training to prepare the birds for performances at the football games.

Cadet falconers receive recognition in a variety of ways. Most important are the sense of satisfaction and the personal recognition they receive from performing the falcons before the general public. Upon selection into the club, each cadet receives from the Commandant of Cadets a distinctive shoulder patch worn on the right shoulder of the blue "A" jacket. The Academy's Personal Development Support Center also presents the second classmen with a minor Air Force letter monogram

Falcon Handler Training

Cadet Arthur O. Compton, Class of 1972, displaying his falcon.
Photo courtesy Office of Public Affairs, Air Force Academy.

after two years in the program. A star is added to the monogram for the first class cadets. The monogram is worn on the right breast of the "A" jacket below the name tag. Additionally, the Athletic Department presents a distinctive white falcon patch, called a "snowy owl" by the cadets, to each handler after completion of his or her third class year. The patch is worn on the "A" jacket on the left breast below the squadron patch. A star is added to the patch after the second class year, and an athletic blanket is given upon graduation.

Cadet falconers all aspire to be selected as the cadet representative for public affairs at an away football game. A senior cadet or two, along with a "hometown" cadet and the public affairs officer, go to the site of the away game on Wednesday or Thursday before the game. They highlight the Academy program and display the falcon for the media, at high schools and other appropriate gatherings. The trip has always proven to be an effective and exciting way to inform the public about the Academy and the privilege is much sought after by the cadets.

Programs for the Air Force—Army and the Air Force—Navy football games. Courtesy Special Collections, Air Force Academy Library.

Training the Performing Mascots

When eyasses (baby falcons) are about eight weeks old, they are "hard penned"—that is, all of their feathers are fully grown and less susceptible to being broken. At this time the birds are removed from the captive-breeding chamber, and an identifying U. S. Fish and Wildlife Service band is put on one leg, and leg bracelets on both legs. Jesses or connecting straps are attached to the bewits (small leather thongs used to attach bells to a falcon) and a swivel and leash are connected to the jesses. The birds are then fitted with a hood and training begins. The hood covers the birds' eyes and they remain quiet when hooded.

The first step involves each falcon handler patiently gaining the confidence and trust of his or her falcon so that it will perch quietly on the "fist." The fist is the heavily gloved (usually the left) hand. This is called "manning" the bird. This initial training requires a minimum of four hours per day for several days. At first the bird, although attached to the fist by the short leash, will "bate"—that is, attempt to fly off the fist—and will need to be assisted back onto the fist. This training continues until the bird becomes calm enough and trusting enough of its handler to eat from his or her other hand while being "manned."

Once this is achieved the training usually progresses well.

The next step involves encouraging the bird to jump first a few inches and then a foot from its perch to the fist to get food. The bird is then required to fly increasing distances from ten to twenty feet from the perch to the falconer's fist. By this time the leash will have been replaced by a creance, which is longer and much like a kite string. The bird then begins to be launched off the fist instead of the perch. After more hours of patient training, the bird will be jumping or flying to a lure instead of to food held in the cadet's hand.

The U.S. Fish and Wildlife Service's falcon identification leg band. Photo courtesy Office of the Director of Falconry, Air Force Academy.

The heavy glove worn by falconers to protect their "fist" from the falcon's claws.
Photo courtesy Office of the Director of Falconry, Air Force Academy.

The lure is a small leather pouch held initially in the hand to which a small piece of meat is attached. The bird soon learns to associate the lure with its food reward. When the bird is flying easily from the fist to the lure, the distance is gradually increased until the bird flies the length of the creance. Finally, when the bird comes off the fist quickly and goes right to the lure every flight, it is time to fly the bird free.

A small transmitter about the size of a thimble with a foot-long antenna attached is placed on one leg with leather bracelets. A bell is attached in the same manner to the other leg. The bird is then released in exactly the same manner as when it was attached to the creance but this time it is free—free to fly away. Initially the bird is given a "straight-in"—that is, it is allowed to hit the lure in a direct straight-in flight from

Typical hoods used to quiet falcons.
Photo courtesy Special Collections, Air Force Academy Library.

Training the Performing Mascots

fist to lure. Then, after a few successful long straight-ins, the lure is pulled away by the cadet falconer just before the bird hits it. This is called a "pass." Typically, the bird will circle around for another attack and the cadet will allow the bird to catch the lure.

The handler's job is to push the bird to longer and longer flights, building stamina for a better show. The handler must be careful not to discourage the bird so that it will become disinterested and fly away. Free-flight training takes another ten days to two weeks for a total of about six to eight weeks. To have a bird performing in front of a crowd usually requires close to ten to twelve weeks of this daily training.

As the football season approaches, the birds are exposed to crowd noise and other distractions so that they will not be frightened and distracted by the first game-day crowd. All during football season the birds are flown, weather permitting, five days a week for training and then on game day until the season ends.

The game-day procedure involves a performance team composed of two birds, each with a handler, and several spotters. One bird is the primary performer and the second a backup in case a problem develops with the primary. The cadet handlers display these birds on the sidelines during the first half of the game. To fly well the birds need to be hungry, so they have been short-rationed the day before (only fed once). Shortly before halftime the backup bird and handler take a position high in the stands where that bird can be released if something goes wrong with the primary. The primary bird is taken to the top of the stadium and positioned so that it can see its handler go to midfield swinging the lure. The primary bird is released and will immediately dive for the lure. The show is on.

The spotters place themselves where they can watch the performing bird in case it flies away. If this happens an immediate search begins to recover the bird. The birds, however, rarely fly away; the few that do are usually recovered. Only six birds have been lost since 1980 and two of these were killed by other birds of prey during training. Before the radio transmitter was brought into use, losses were more frequent. The device has greatly assisted recovery.

A falcon "bating" off Cadet Mark Abbott's fist. Photo by Cadet Steve Roscio. Courtesy Special Collections, Air Force Academy Library.

Lure and creance line. Courtesy Special Collections, Air Force Academy Library.

Cadet Mark Abbott's falcon about to leave the perch for his fist.

The falcon leaves its perch to take the bait from Cadet Mark Abbott's hand.

Falcon lands on Cadet Mark Abbott's fist for the first time.
All photos by Cadet Roscio. Courtesy Special Collections, Air Force Academy Library.

Training the Performing Mascots

The Air Force Academy is very proud of its falconry program. It has taken many years of work and the assistance of many skilled individuals and organizations to achieve the successful, self-sustaining program in existence today. It is unique among the many national and international programs dealing with birds of prey. Most, if not all, other programs and individual enthusiasts are training birds to hunt, rehabilitating injured or sick birds, offering static displays, or retraining birds to return to the wild. To be able to conduct free-flight demonstrations of wild birds is indeed a tribute to the dedication, the careful planning, and patient training by the staff and cadets of the Falconry Club.

A falcon attached to the creance flying to the lure. Photo courtesy Office of the Director of Falconry, Air Force Academy.

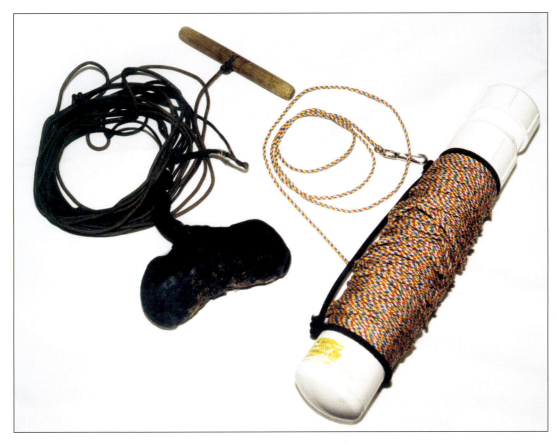

The lure and creance line on which the birds are first trained. Photo by MSgt. Kenneth L. Carter. Courtesy Special Collections, Air Force Academy Library.

A falcon flying free to the lure. Photo courtesy Office of the Director of Falconry, Air Force Academy.

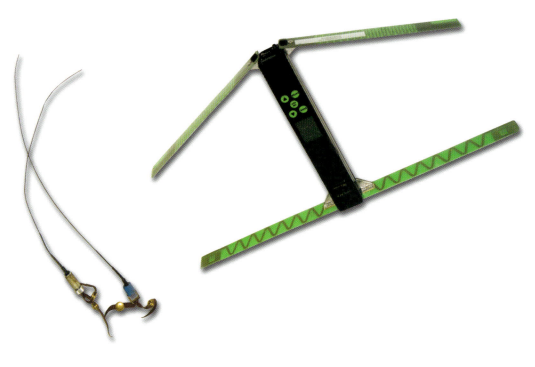

Basic telemetering receiver with the transmitter that is attached to the falcon. Photo courtesy Office of the Director of Falconry, Air Force Academy.

Training the Performing Mascots

A falcon flying free to the lure in Falcon Stadium at the Air Force Academy.
Photo courtesy Office of the Director of Falconry, Air Force Academy.

Public Affairs

Through the falconry program's public exhibits and flight demonstrations of the Academy mascot, the American people have been given an important opportunity to see a highly visible and interesting aspect of the life of the Academy. The Falconry Club is one of the Academy's official performing units and its members are active in the Academy's Speakers Bureau as well as handling many tours and presentations at the mews where the birds are kept. The cadet falconers are very effective representatives wherever they appear with their falcons. In 1999 the falconry program won the Air Force–wide public affairs excellence award.

Performance records are impressive. Since 1979 the Falconry Club has made over 150 public appearances per year. By the late 1990s that number had grown to almost 500 per year. Each year since 1987 the falcons have been presented in performance flights about thirty-five times. During any given year, the cadet falconers display their birds in ten to thirteen different states. Civic groups,

Cadet James Ryan, Class of 2000, displaying his falcon to a group on a public affairs trip. Photo courtesy Office of Public Affairs, Air Force Academy.

Superintendent Lt. Gen. A. P. Clark with *Baffin* in 1973. Photo courtesy Office of Public Affairs, Air Force Academy.

school classes, scout units, and church organizations enjoy interacting with the cadet falconers and learning about the story of the selection of the falcon as the Academy mascot, the types of falcons, their training as performers, and the captive-breeding program. These presentations include the display of a live bird, questions from the audience, a photo opportunity, and often a chance to actually touch the falcon.

In mid-October 1955, while the program was still in its infancy, Col. Max B. Boyd, Academy Director of Information, raised an interesting question. The first official mascot, **Mach I,** was a female. Colonel Boyd suggested that a male mascot would be more appropriate. This "macho" suggestion must be viewed in light of the fact that it was made twenty-one years before the first female cadets were admitted to the Academy. **Mach I** was "a bird in hand and she was worth two in the bush," so no attempt was made to replace her. Thus, the official decision was "to make no issue over the sex of the Academy mascot." Actually, the male falcon is more agile, has less wing span, and is more maneuverable; by 1999 most of the performing birds were male.

On October 20, 1956, the Academy's falcons made their first public demonstration at halftime of the football game between the Academy and the Colorado School of Mines at Denver University stadium. This exciting event was recorded in the Falconry Club's history:

> As an announcement was made over the public address system, Cadet Thom walked out onto the football field the lure back over his shoulder and gauntlet on his fist. At the same time, Cadet Frey carried Lucifer high into the stands and removed his leash and swivel. Cadet Melancon, with Castor, was located at the north end of the stadium, ready to release his bird in the event of a mishap with Lucifer. Lucifer's hood was "struck," and as Cadet Thom began to swing the lure, the hood was removed. For a breathtaking moment, nothing happened, and then the tiercel was gone, driving hard, low over the heads of the crowd, towards the lure.
>
> There was some yelling from the Colorado School of Mines students even though the spectators had been requested to make no noise. This demonstration did not appear to affect the tiercel. After the first stoop (dive), he pitched up over the east stands, turned and came back in again; as he did so, the stands fell silent and no further disturbance was heard.
>
> During the course of the flight, a pigeon flew across the stadium and was completely ignored by the bird, intent on the lure. Later, experience showed that none of the Academy birds, trained on the inanimate lure from the time they could fly, would pay more than passing attention to a pigeon, but on this occasion it

Public Affairs

was a distinct relief to see the pigeon pass unchallenged.

In all, six or eight stoops were made, although it seemed like more. Finally, Cadet Thom threw the lure in the air and gave the normal shout. The tiercel attacked it in mid-flight and settled to the ground. As Lucifer hit the lure, there was a burst of spontaneous applause throughout the stadium, a very rewarding gesture to the cadets who had worked so hard to bring the demonstration to reality.

From then on, the falcons were a feature of every Academy football game.

A cadet with his falcon performing in Falcon Stadium at a football game. Photo courtesy Office of the Director of Falconry, Air Force Academy.

Conclusion

When the Academy cadets chose the falcon to be their mascot, they broke new ground in the long history of college and university mascots because the falcon was the first collegiate mascot (and a wild creature at that) to perform at sports events, free and untethered.

While the Academy's falconry program met very effectively a traditional sports and public relations function, it was more than that. The falcon with its swift and graceful flight, aggressive spirit, and noble bearing epitomizes the Air Force mission. Indeed, one of the premiere U.S. Air Force fighter-bombers of the 1980s and 1990s, the F-16, is called the Fighting Falcon. What more suitable icon could there be to inspire the future leaders of the Air Force? Additionally, the falconry program, which each year introduces new cadet bird handlers and new young birds to this ancient sport, is known, studied, and respected by falconers everywhere. Indeed, many of the most distinguished among them have contributed in one way or another to the current robust status of the Academy's program. Finally, the impressive way in which upper class cadets introduce new cadets to the program and inspire them to devote most of their spare time to the care, training, display, and performance of these birds for four years has earned for the program the status of a leadership laboratory.

In summary, this program is one of a kind and reflects the vitality and diversity of the activities in which cadets are involved at the Academy. It has introduced into the sports programs a sense of the rich history of falconry and has added interest and vitality to the Academy's leadership training and to its public image.

APPENDICES

***Aurora*, the gyrfalcon mascot of the Air Force Academy, in 2001.** Photography by MSgt. Kenneth L. Carter. Courtesy Special Collections, Air Force Academy Library.

Officers-in-Charge (OICs)/ Directors of the Academy Falconry Program

Capt. Harrison H. D. Heiberg, Jr., 30 Sep 55–July 57; from the Office of the Commandant of Cadets.

Maj. William L. Richardson, Jr., July 57–May 60; from the Department of History.

Maj. Donald W. Galvin, May 60–June 63; from the Department of Political Science.

Capt. Charles H. Milian, June 63–July 65; from Cadet Military Training.

Col. James C. McIntyre, July 65–Dec 75; Command Veterinarian. The Academy mews is named in his honor.

Maj. Manuel A. Thomas, Dec 75–Aug 79; Command Veterinarian.

Capt. Gerry M. Henningsen, Aug 79–Mar 81; Command Veterinarian.

Col. Lawrence E. Schaad, Mar 81–June 95; Command Veterinarian.

Maj. James R. Riddle, June 95–July 97; Command Veterinarian.

Maj. Timothy S. Wells, July 97–July 99; from the Cadet Clinic.

Maj. Timothy Woodruff, July 99–July 2002; Commander Public Health Office.

Lt. Col. Steven Niehoff, Aug 2002– ; Commander Public Health Office.

Roster of First Class Cadet Falcon Handlers 1959–2003

Class of 1959
Frederick E. Frey
Did not graduate but was first cadet to fly a falcon to the lure.
John M. Melancon
Kenneth S. Thom
Did not graduate but was first cadet to fly a falcon performing at a football game.

Class of 1960
Had no graduate bird handlers

Class of 1961
Terry J. Guess
George T. Nolde, Jr.

Class of 1962
Harry G. Paddon, III
Daryl P. Wood

Class of 1963
Merrill E. Eastcott, Jr.
Harry M. Juister
Relva L. Lilly

Class of 1964
Alfred J. Mateczun, Jr.
Fred V. McClintock
James M. Wood

Class of 1965
Joseph O. Blacksten, II
Victor L. Genez
Michael D. Muldoon
Allen F. Natella
Peter G. Pfendler

Class of 1966
James E. Meadows
Edward A. Petersen, III
John R. Wormington

Class of 1967
Jonathan L. Hicks
Glenn W. Lund
David V. Nowlin
Arnold W. Tan

Class of 1968
James R. Bettcher
James L. Hazen
Fredrick J. Hernlem, III
V. Seth Jensen
Marion A. Marshall
Charles T. Robertson, Jr.

Class of 1969
John A. Hinchey
Arthur B. Polnisch, Jr.
Darrel D. Whitcomb

Class of 1997
Ryan A. Campbell
Joshua S, Johnson
Stacy A. Kreuziger

Class of 1998
Carl E. Haney
Rebekah G. Leivers
Shawna R. Ng-A-Qui

Class of 1999
Matthew H. Beverly
Daniel G. Hendrix
Matthew C. Stanley

Class of 2000
Isham F. Barrett
Christopher P. Knier
James M. Ryan, IV

Class of 2001
Trevor N. Hall
Annahita M. Marefat
Ronald E. Palmer
Malcolm S. Schongalla
Matthew J. Ziemann

Class of 2002
John D. Edwards
Peter J. Mauro
Mark A. Melin
Steven Morris

Class of 2003
Courtney B. Hancock
Luke J. Rostowfske
Ashley P. Watson

Glossary

Terms, Acronyms, and Expressions

Accipiter—short-winged hawk of classic falconry

Air show—an open house at an airport during which the public is invited to see a variety of aviation-related activities

Air strike program—an activity to minimize midair collisions between wild birds and aircraft by frightening them away from the airfield using trained falcons

Apprenticeship—a period during which a prospective falconer understudies a licensed falconer

Appropriated fund—funds provided by Congress instead of obtained by a revenue-producing activity

Bates, Bating—refers to the act of a bird of prey jumping or attempting to fly from a gloved fist, or perch/block, to which it is fastened by a short tether, but falling down and pulling itself up to the original position

Bell—in falconry context, a small bell used to locate falcons

Bewits—small leather thongs by which bells are attached as falconry hardware to safely restrain a bird of prey

Bird Air Strike—the term referring to a manmade object (e.g., aircraft) being hit by a bird

Block—a perch on which a falcon can be permanently kept with a tether

Braces, traces—leather straps used to open/close a hood

Breeder pen—the enclosure housing breeding falcons; contains perches, a nest ledge, and windows open to the outdoors

Breeders—falcons used solely to produce young

Brooding—the process by which young birds are kept warm, either naturally by parent birds, or artificially by heat lamps to allow the young birds to grow and become stronger

Cadet-in-Charge (CIC)—a new senior (first class) cadet elected by those falconers from the class about to graduate to lead the other falconers during the forthcoming year

Candle(s)—to view an egg over a high intensity light and gently rotating the egg to observe the silhouette of an embryo in the egg

Captive breeding—the practice of breeding wild birds or animals in captivity

Captive-breeding permit—the authorization issued by federal or state authorities to carry out captive breeding of wild birds or animals

Carrion—dead flesh eaten by scavengers

Carry—to keep a falcon on the fist for a prolonged period in training

Cast—flying two birds to a single lure

Chicken—in the falconry program context, five-to six-week old chickens fed to falcons after gutting and trimming off feet and heads

Clutch—a collection of four to six eggs making up the set of eggs to be incubated by the parent birds

Cockrel—a rooster chicken, raised as food for the falcons

Cope, Coping—the process of trimming the beak or talons of a falcon

Coturnix quail—Japanese quail formerly raised at the Air Force Academy to feed the falcons

Creance—a long line of heavy "kite" string used to physically restrain falcons early in their flight training

Double clutching—the process whereby man can artificially alter the falcons' egg-laying process so that two separate sets of eggs are laid, the second beginning two weeks after the first set is removed from the nest

DOW (Division of Wildlife)—Colorado state agency that monitors the Academy falconry program

Evidence bird—an injured, stolen, or abused bird that has been confiscated and is being held at the Air Force Academy mews at the request of the United States Fish and Wildlife Service (USFWS) for use as evidence in a court case

Eyass, eyasses—a young falcon or falcons (a chick)

Eyrie—a nest site

Falcon—a long-winged, dark-eyed bird of prey; or a female falcon, as opposed to the male falcon which is called a tiercel

Falconry licensing examination—a test administered by the Colorado DOW covering laws, physiology, housing, and care of birds of prey; qualifies a person who passes this test with a score of 80 percent or better to be a licensed falconer

Fed up—term referring to gorging a bird of prey with all the food it can eat, often over 20 percent of its weight

Fertile—an egg which, if properly incubated, has a good chance of yielding a baby bird

Fledge—refers to a young falcon becoming old enough to be on its own, not dependent on its parents

Food ration—the measured amount of food—raw meat, whole animal (including feather or fur, bone, and muscle)—which will be a falcon's supply of food for one day; usually about 10 percent of its weight

Foster—refers to a process by which young peregrine falcon parents take care of falcon babies not their own so that the parenting instinct in the adults is strengthened

Gauntlet—glove with wide cuff used to hold bird of prey while protecting the handler

Graduation—the Air Force Academy graduation day is the Wednesday morning after the Memorial Day weekend

Glossary

Gyrfalcon—the largest and most noble of the falcons; the white-phase gyrfalcon is the official mascot of the Air Force Academy

Haggard—an adult bird of prey

Hand raised—to patiently and calmly condition a bird of prey to being around people; not taming but calming the bird down

Hard penned—referring to feathers that are fully grown, with quills clear, no longer blood-filled; a bird that is hard penned is less likely to break these tougher feathers than one "in the blood," that is, still growing

Hawk—a bird of prey with short wings, light-colored eyes

Hood—a close fitting leather cap used to cover the head and eyes of a bird of prey

Husbandry—the practice of providing quality housing, food, and care to an animal or bird species

Hybrid—the cross mixing of two species

Imprinting—the term referring to a young bird associating with other living objects (e.g., people) and thinking that they are its parents instead of another bird of its same species

Jess, Jesses—the leather strap connected to a permanent leather bracelet to restrain a bird of prey

Kestrel—the smallest falcon in North America; also called the sparrow hawk or wind hover

Leadership laboratory—a term referring to an activity at the Air Force Academy in which cadets practice skills of leadership they have learned in class

Leash—a detachable leather thong attached to the jesses by a swivel with which a trained bird of prey is restrained

Lure—an artificial "quarry" to which is attached food and which the falcon considers to be a "dinner plate" when it sees the lure

Lure bag—the handler's satchel containing the lure, food, and other equipment used when flying a falcon

Manned, Manning—calming a falcon to the point where it will stand quietly on the handler's fist

Merlin—the second smallest falcon in North America

Mews—the building where falcons are housed

Mews Watch—the summer program during which cadet falconers train recently fledged baby falcons in preparation for the upcoming football season

Molt—the annual shedding of feathers by a bird of prey; occurs from about April through October each year after the first year of the bird's life

Officer-in-Charge (OIC)—the officer with overall responsibility of managing a cadet program, in this case the falconry program

On-season—refers to the period during the Academy year when a specific group of cadets is assigned to train and to handle the falcons on a daily basis; all cadet falconers are "on-season" during the fall (football) season and either winter or spring season

Parenting instinct—refers to the extent to which an adult bird demonstrates the ability to be a good parent

Peregrine falcon—the second largest and fastest of the falcons; formerly an endangered species in the United States

Possession permit—the granting of permission by the USFWS and Colorado DOW to possess birds of prey or taxidermy mounts

Prairie falcon—the middle-sized falcon of the five types found in North America; common in the Rocky Mountains; selected to be the performing mascot at the Air Force Academy; captively raised at the Academy since 1974

Predator—a bird or animal that hunts other birds or animals for food

President's Weekend—Commemoration at the Academy of Washington's and Lincoln's birthdays, mid-February

Prey base—the amount and quality of food available in the wild to a predator or, in this case, bird of prey

Public relations—an organized staff effort to share information and activities with the local community

Quarry—the game being hunted by birds of prey

Raptor—any of the birds of prey—hawks, falcons, eagles, owls

Rehabilitation—the healing of sick or injured wild birds or animals for eventual return to the wild

Richardson's merlin—a subspecies of merlin

Scrape—a depression in gravel that becomes the nest of a falcon and into which eggs are laid

Set(s)—refers to placing eggs into an incubator

Spotters—cadet falconers or OICs who watch the direction in which a performing falcon may fly away to facilitate tracking and recovery

Stock—refers to birds used for breeding as in breeding stock

Stoop—the head-first dive of a falcon from a height in attacking prey or a lure

Strike—contact between falcon and lure

Strike (the hood)—open the braces of the hood

Summer (Academy)—from graduation until the start of classes in early August; divided into three, approximately three-week long periods

Swivel—a metal device used to connect the jesses with the leash or creance on a falcon's leg to keep it from getting tangled

Talon—falcon's toenail

Team chief—the senior cadet in charge of each group of three falcon handlers responsible for the training of a performing mascot

Tiercel—a male falcon, the smaller of the sexes

Transmitter—the radio telemetry equipment part which is attached to the falcons when flying free in training or in performing; enables the bird to be tracked and recovered if it should fly away

Glossary

Tundra peregrine—a subspecies of the peregrine falcon

USFWS (United States Fish and Wildlife Service)—the federal agency which monitors the Air Force Academy's falconry program in conjunction with the Colorado Division of Wildlife

Venison—deer meat which, in the early days of the Academy falconry program, was fed to the falcons

Weather, weathering—to place falcons in the open air in good weather

Weathering pen—the enclosure used to house falcons in the open air in good weather to protect them from predators

Academy Library Resources and Selected Bibliography

Following the inception of the cadet falconry program, the staff of the Academy Library directed by Col. (later Brig. Gen.) George V. Fagan began to compile a collection of materials related to falcons and falconry. The materials include books, periodical literature, pamphlets, dissertations and theses, government documents (e.g., public laws and regulations, legislative hearings), technical reports, special studies, selected art works, novels, poetry, and a collection of falconry accouterments.

With holdings dating from the sixteenth century, the Library's falconry collection is considered to be one of the most significant in the nation. The collection supports the Academy's falconry program with publications ranging from beginner's guides to in-depth studies on the art of falconry. It includes volumes in Italian, French, and German, as well as English. The early works clearly show that the sport of falconry was limited to royalty and aristocracy. Several of the volumes are quite rare, and others, because of their accuracy and detail, are known and respected throughout the international community of falconry. An example of one of the rarest volumes is *De arte venandi cum avibus* (The Art of Falconry) by Frederick II of Hohenstaufen (1194—1250 A.D.), Holy Roman Emperor; first published in Berlin in 1896.

To preserve the integrity of the collection and to protect the rare items it contains, falconry materials are housed in the Library's Special Collections Branch. All of the holdings are listed as

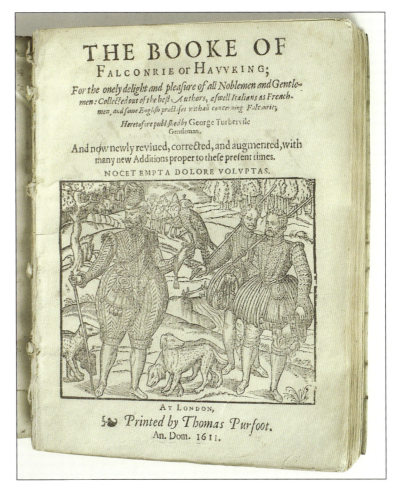

17th century treatise on the art of falconry from the Air Force Academy Library collection.
Courtesy Special Collections, Air Force Academy Library.

a separate topic in the Academy Library's special bibliography series. The bibliography is periodically updated and the most recent edition (1990) contains over 1,200 entries. Single copies of the Academy Library bibliography are available by writing to the Director of Air Force Academy Libraries, 2354 Fairchild Drive, USAF Academy, CO 80840-5701. The following is a representative selection of the many titles listed in the Air Force Academy Library Special Bibliography Series, No. 81, Falconry:

Abbott, Mark J. "US Air Force Academy Falconry," Unpublished manuscript, United States Air Force Academy, 1981.

Ap Evans, Humphrey. *Falconry for You.* London: J. Gifford, [1960]. *A good, modern introduction to the working aspects of the sport.*

Beebe, Frank Lyman. *A Falconry Manual.* Surry, B. C.; Blaine, Wash.: Hancock House, c1984.

———. *Hawks, Falcons, Falconry.* Saanichton, B. C.; Seattle, Wash.: Hancock House, 1976. *An in-depth look by one of the foremost falconers of falconry, training techniques, and husbandry.*

——— and H. M. Webster. *North American Falconry and Hunting Hawks.* Denver, Colo.: North American Falconry and Hunting Hawks, 1964. *Probably the best volume printed on falconry; updated in 1985, including chapters by U. S. Air Force Academy falconry consultant, Dr. James H. Enderson.*

Bert, Edmund. *Treatise of Hawks and Hawking.* [n. p. 1950]. Reprint of original 1619 edition. *The classic work on shortwinged hawks. Old, but based on much experience. Ignore the remedies.*

Blaine, Gilbert. *Falconry.* Newton, Mass.: Branford, [1970]. Reprint of the 1936 edition. *By a specialist in training/hunting with eyass, longwinged hawks.*

Bodio, Stephen. *A Rage for Falcons.* New York: Schocken Books, 1984. *An entertaining narrative about falconry by one who practices the art, and a good layman's introduction—conveying the why, rather than the "how-to" of the sport.*

The Booke of Falconrie or Hawking: For the onely delight and pleasure of all Noblemen and Gentlemen. London, Printed by Thomas Purfoot, 1611.

Broderick, William. *Falconers' favorites,* by W. Broderick. London: Printed by Taylor Francis for John Van Voorst, 1865. *Contains beautiful color prints of falcons.*

Burton, Philip John Kennedy. *Birds of Prey.* New York: Gallery Books, 1989. *A comprehensive volume of the world's raptors (birds of prey) with color prints and detailed information on the natural history of these birds.*

Cade, Tom J. *The Falcons of the World.* Ithaca, N. Y.: Comstock/Cornell University Press, 1982. *An extensive study and beautiful depiction of the birds by the leading falconer/scientist/raptor specialist in the world.*

California Hawking Club. *A Beginner's Manual of Falconry.* Davis, Calif.: California Hawking Club, 1965. Revised periodically. *Excellent guidance for the beginning practitioner.*

Clark, William S. *A Field Guide to Hawks, North America.* Boston: Houghton Mifflin, 1987. *A superb identification guide to birds of prey.*

Cooper, John E. *Veterinary Aspects of Captive Birds of Prey with 1985 Supplement.* 2d rev. ed. Gloucestershire, England: Standfast Press, 1985. *The foremost volume on veterinary care and treatment of birds of prey.*

Coursing and Falconry. Southampton: Ashford Press, 1986. Facsim. of ed. published London: Longman, 1892. Coursing by Harding Cox; falconry by Gerald Lascelles. *By specialists in training/hunting with passage, longwinged hawks.*

Fisher, Charles Hawkins. *Reminiscences of a Falconer.* London: J. C Nimmo, 1901.

Frederick II, Holy Roman Emperor. *The Art of Falconry: Being the De arte venandi cum avibus of Frederick II of Hohenstaufen.* Boston: C. T. Branford, 1955. Also published by the Stanford University Press, 1943. *One of the first and most complete documentations of the art in the Western world. Frederick II lived from 1194–1250 A.D. De arte venandi cum avibus was first published in Berlin in 1896.*

Freeman, Gage Earle. *Falconry, Its Claims, History and Practice.* London: Longman, Green, Longman, and Roberts, 1859.

Game Hawking—At Its Very Best: A Falconry Anthology. Denver, Colo.: Windsong Press, 1988. *Details of the various aspects of hunting with trained raptors, each described by a trained practitioner. Includes advertisements for falconry equipment and works of art.*

Glasier, Phillip. *Falconry and Hawking.* 2d ed. London: Batsford, 1986. *A comprehensive look at training of falconry birds.*

Harting, James Edmund. *Hints on the Management of Hawks and Practical Falconry: Chapters Historical and Descriptive.* 2d ed. Maidenhead, England: Thames Valley Press, 1971. *An update of one of the original books on falconry—much practical information on the basics of the sport.*

Latham, Simon. *Lathams Falconry: or, The Faulcons Lure, and Cure in Two Bookes.* Amsterdam: Theatrum Orbis Terrarum; Norwood, N. J.: W. J. Johnson, 1976. Photoreprint of the 1615 ed.; printed by I. B. for R. Jackson. *The classic work on long-winged hawks. Ignore the remedies.*

Mavrogordato, Jack. *A Falcon in the Field: A Treatise on the Training and Flying of Falcons Being a Companion Volume and Sequel to a Hawk for the Bush.* London: Knightly Vernon, 1966.

———. *A Hawk for the Bush: A Treatise on the Training of the Sparrow-hawk and other Short-winged Hawks.* New York: C. N. Potter; distributed by Crown Publishers, [1973]. *Written on training the European sparrowhawk but, in fact, a very insightful modern work on flying all the shortwinged hawks.*

McElroy, Harry C. *Desert Hawking.* [Yuma, Ariz: Cactus Press, n.d.].

———. *Desert Hawking* II. Tucson: McElroy, 1996. *Especially valuable for description of Harris hawks in falconry—not included in the earlier literature.*

McGranaghan, L. J. *The Red-tailed Hawk* 2nd ed., 1997, c1996. Privately printed. *A good treatment of this important bird in American falconry, a species not otherwise well-covered.*

Michell, Edward Blair. *The Art and Practice of Hawking.* Boston, Mass.: C. T. Branford, 1959. First published 1900. *More than normal detail; by a merlin specialist, but good for hawking with all species of hawks.*

New York Department of Environmental Conservation Division of Fish and Wildlife. *New York State Falconry Examination Manual.* Albany, N. Y.: New York State, Dept. of Environmental Conservation, [1987]. Periodically reissued. *Excellent guidance for preparation for the examination required to obtain a falconry license.*

Newton, Ian. *Population Ecology of Raptors.* Vermillion, S. D.: Buteo Books, 1979.

Oakes, W. C. *The Falconer's Apprentice.* Elizabeth, Colo.: EagleWing, 1993. *A must for anyone beginning in the sport. Goes beyond the how-to in an important discussion of ethics.*

O'Brien, Dan. *The Rites of Autumn: A Falconer's Journey Across the American West.* New York: Atlantic Monthly Press, 1988. *Good readable introduction, especially with respect to the esthetics of the sport; a good feel for falconers and falconry.*

Palmer, Ralph S. *Handbook of North American Birds.* New Haven, Conn.: Yale University Press, 1962. *Outstanding, detailed account of all the diurnal raptors. Good preparation for the examination required to obtain a falconry license.*

Peeters, Hans J. *American Hawking: A General Account of Falconry in the New World.* Davis, Calif., 1970. *Good look at contemporary American falconry.*

Peregrine Falcon Populations: Their Biology and Decline. Madison: University of Wisconsin Press, 1969. *Papers and discussions of a conference on the subject held by the University of Wisconsin from 29 August to 1 September 1965.*

Rowley, Sam R. *Discovering Falconry: A Comprehensive Guide to Contemporary Falconry.* Colorado Springs, Colo.: New Dawn Publications, 1985. *An excellent beginner's book on falconry.*

Salvin, Francis Henry. *Falconry in the British Isles.* London: J. van Voorst, 1855.

Samson, Jack. *Falconry Today.* New York: H. Z. Walck, 1976. *Another excellent book for the beginning falconer.*

Schlegel, Hermann. *Traite de fauconnerie.* [Denver, Colo.: Chasse Publications, 1973]. Leiden Arnz, 1844–53. Reprint of the original edition with English translation by Thomas J. Hanlon.

Snow, Carol. *Gyrfalcon, Falco rusticolus* L. Denver, Colo.: Bureau of Land Management, U. S. Department of the Interior, Denver Service Center, 1974. *An in-depth study of the gyrfalcon.*

———. *Prairie Falcon, Falco mexicanus.* Denver, Colo.: Bureau of Land Management, U.S. Department of the Interior, Denver Service Center, 1974. *An in-depth study of the prairie falcon.*

Snyder, Noel, and Helen Snyder. *Birds of Prey: Natural History and Conservation of North American Raptors.* Voyageur Press, 1991.

Stevens, Ronald. *Observations on Modern Falconry.* Saskatoon, B. C.: Falconiforme Press, 1978. *One of the best discussions on modern falconry by an astute and sensitive modern falconer.*

For young readers:

Arnold, Caroline. *Saving the Peregrine Falcon.* Minneapolis, Minn.: Carolrhoda Books, 1985. *A well-illustrated description of peregrine falcons, their plight because of DDT, and the efforts involved in captive breeding and raising of peregrines.*

George, Jean Craighead. *On the Far Side of the Mountain.* New York: Dutton Children's Books, 1990. *A wonderful adventure, sequel to* My Side of the Mountain *made famous as a motion picture.*

———. *The Summer of the Falcon.* New York: Harper Row, 1979, c1962. *An adventure story of a child training a kestrel.*

Graham, Ada. *Falcon Flight.* New York: Delacorte Press, 1978. *A narrative about falconry, but especially of the peregrine's reduction in numbers and what was done to bring them back from extinction.*

Murphy, Robert William. *The Peregrine Falcon.* Boston: Houghton Mifflin, 1964. *A novel depicting a period of time in the life of a peregrine falcon.*

White, T. H. *The Goshawk.* New York: Putnam, 1952; London: Longmans, 1964. *An adventure story about a man training a hawk. How not to train a goshawk. A compelling insight into the feelings of the falconer—great literature, despite the author's falconry errors.*

Index

(*Note*: Page numbers in **bold** indicate pictures.)

Abbott, Mark, **38, 49, 50**
Air Force Academy. *See* United States Air Force Academy
Amanda, 14
Aplomados, 3
Apollo XV, 15
Arizona-Sonora Desert Museum, 14, 28
Arnold, R. W., **17**
Athena, 14
Athol, 14
Aurora, 14, **61**
Aztecs, 1

Baffin, 14, **56**
Bald Eagle Act, 11
Bartles, 15–16
Bating, 47, **49**
Beebe, Frank L., 13, 20; *North American Falconry and Hunting Hawks*, 20, 27
Belle, 28
Bells, **41,** 48
Bewits, 47
Bird Strike Program (U.S. Air Force), 21–22
Birds of prey. *See* Raptors
Birds of Prey Rehabilitation Foundation, 21
Blizzard, 14, 34
The Booke of Falconrie or Hawking, **75**
Boyd, Max B., 56
Bracelets, 47
Breeding, 27–28; difficulties, 28–29; facilities, 29–30; initial efforts, 28, 33; pen, **27;** program, 28, 33
Bumblefoot, 14
Burgess, Woodbury, 9
Burnett, Chuck, **38**

Calgary Zoo, 16
Cannone, Anthony, **42**
Captain Helene, 13
Carnie, S. Kent, 20, **20**
Castor, 15

Cecchine, Dan L., Jr., 20
Central Asia, 1
Cheyenne Mountain Zoo, 21
Chickens, 31
China, 1
Clark, A. P., **56**
Cody, 16, **16**
Colorado Aspen Center for Environmental Studies, 21
Colorado Division of Wildlife, 14, 16, 20–21, 25, 29, 38; raptor licensing, 39
Colorado School of Mines, 15, 56–57
Compton, Arthur O., **45**
Cortez, 1
Crawford, Walter, 20
Creances, 47, **51**

Darian, 16
DDT, 21
De arte venandi cum avibus, 75
DeKalb Hatchery, 31
Deluca, Mark, 38
The Denver Post, 12
Denver University, 13, 56–57
Dollar, William S. (Sam), 20, 22, 29

Eagles, 11
Egypt, 1
Eisenhower, Dwight D., 15
Enderson, James H., 14, 20, 22; as consultant to falconry program, 27–28
Europe, 1

F-16 Fighting Falcon, **viii,** 59; lapel pin, 29
Facilities. *See* Mews. *See also under* Breeding
Fagan, George V., 75
Falconry, **x,** 1, **34;** Academy Library collection on, 75–76; Arabia, **xii,** 1; and European nobility, 1; as "sport of kings," 1; flying to the lure, 1–2, 2, 49, **52, 53**

81

Falconry Club (AFA), 9, 14–15, 16–17, 51, 59; assistant OICs, 37–38, 43; association with athletic department, 37; and athletic events, 41, 43; beginnings, 37; cadets-in-charge (CIC), 37–38, 44; contributions to falconry, 33–34; fall season, 43; first demonstration, 56–57; group photos, **38, 40, 42**; handlers and spotters, 49, 65–68; leadership training, 38–39; letter monogram, 44–45, **44**; member selection, 39–40; officers-in-charge (OIC), 37–38, 41, 43, 44, 63; operation, 38; performance and display, 41, 44, 49, 51, 55–57, **55, 57**; public affairs, 55–57; roster (1959–2003), 65–68; shoulder patches, **43**, 44–45; spring season, 44; summer Mews Watch, 44; time commitment, 41, 43; veterinarians as OICs, 27; winter season, 43–44

Falconry Club of America, 9

Falconry program. See Falconry Club (AFA)

Falcons, **vi**, 3–4, **10**; characteristics, 3–4; eyesight, 3; hard penned, 47; hunting with (see Falconry); North American species, 3; performance and display, 41, 44, 49, 51, 55–57, **55, 57**; raising to maturity, 30; rehabilitation programs, 20, 21–22, 33; selection as mascot for USAFA, 9–12, 59; . See also Aplomados, Gyrfalcons, Kestrels, Merlins, Peregrines, Prairie falcons

Feeding, 31

Finkenstadt, Chris, **42**

Finley, Mike, **38**

Fixemer, Joe, **42**

Flavin, John, 15, 19–20

Flying Training Squadron patch, **28**

Football game programs, **46**

France, 1

Frederick II, Holy Roman Emperor, 75

Frey, Frederick E., 13, 41, 56

Galvin, Donald R., 9

Gaus, Arnold, **38**

Girton, Wendy, **39**

Glacier, **4**, 14, **38**

Glossary, 69–73

Gloves, 47, **48**

Goetze, Richard B., 13

Graham, Richard, 14

Gyrfalcons, **viii**, 3, 4, **4**, 13–14, **61**; Academy as repository for, 33

Halliwell, William H., 20

Harmon, Hubert R., 9, 12

Havoc, 29

Hawking, 1

Hawks, 3

Heddinger, Mike, **42**

Heiberg, Harrison H. D., Jr., 12, 15, 19, **19**, 23; establishment of official status for falcon handlers, 37

Henningsen, Gerry, 14

Herd, Kim, **42**

Hoods, **11, 16, 47, 48**

Houdini, 14, 28

Hungry, 15

India, 1

Japan, 1

Jaymes, 15–16

Jesses, 47

Jezebel, 15

Jock, 15

Johnson, R. K., **17**

Karger, John, 20

Kestrels, 3, 5, **5**, 16, 33, **42, 84**

Kris, 13

Kris II, 13

Last Chance Forever Organization, 20, 21

Lewis, Peter, **38**

Lil, 33–34

Lowry Air Force Base, 25, **26**, 37

Lucifer, 15, **15**, 41, 56–57

Lure, 48, 49, **51**; flying to, 1–2, 2, 49, **52, 53**; training to fly to, 47–49

Mach I, 13, **13**, 14, 41, 56

Mascots, 9–12, 59

Massachusetts Institute of Technology, 9

Maximus, 16

McIntyre, James C., 20, **21**, 25–26; and captive breeding, 27, 33; and feeding practices, 31; and raptor rehabilitation, 21, 33

McIntyre Mews. See Mews

Melancon, John M., 56

Meredith, Russell "Luff," 9, **9**, 13, 19

Merlins, 3, 5, 5, 16; Academy as repository for, 33

Mews, 23, 25–26, 26; breeding pen, 27; classroom, 23; construction of, 25; drainage, 24; electricity, 24; food storage, 24; Mews Watch, 44; security, 24; space needs,

Index

Mews, *continued*
23–24; storage and work rooms, 24; tours, 44; water needs, 24; weathering pen, **25**
Milo, 15
Muller, Dennis, **42**

Nellis Air Force Base, 21–22
Niehoff, Steve, **42**
Nike, 15
North American Falconry and Hunting Hawks, 20, 27

Patrick, 16
Peltzer, Krysta, **42**
Peregrine Fund, 22, 28; donation of quail, 31; and incubation of eggs, 30
Peregrines, 3, 4, 12, 13, 14–15, 16; Academy as repository for, 33; baby eyasses, **30;** and breeding, 28, 29; as endangered species, 21, 22; pictures, **4, 42;** subtypes, 14
Performance and display, 41, 44, 49, 51, 55–57, **55, 57**
Persia, 1
Phoenix, 14, 29, 33–34
Pollux, 15
Postlewaite, Richard, **38**
Prairie falcons, 3, 4–5, 15–16, 22; and breeding, 28, 29; hatching of eyasses, 44; pictures, **5, 42;** protected status in Colorado, 25; training and molting, 41
Preventive medicine, 33

Quail, 22, 31

Radio transmitters, 48, 49, **52**
Raptor Rehabilitation and Propagation Project, 20, 21
Raptors, 1, 11; captive breeding, 27; molting, 41–43; rehabilitation, 20, 21, 33
Rath, Brian, **38**
Richardson, William L., Jr., 15
Ryan, James, **55**

Sara, 34
Saudi Arabia, King of, gift of falcons, **17**
Schaad, Lawrence E., 20, **20,** 29, **38**
Scott, D. R., 15

Scott, W. W., Jr., 16
Sharp, Dudley C., 17
Skip, 16
Smith, Pat, **38**
Soraya, 14, 34
Stabler, Robert M., 15, 20
Stillman, Robert M., 9–10
Stone, William S., **17**
Stoop, 3–4

Terminology, 69–73
Thom, Kenneth S., 15, **15,** 41, 56–57
Thunder, 16
Titanium, 16
Training, 27, 41–43, 44; equipment, 47; to fly to the lure, 47–49; to jump or fly to the fist, 47, **50;** launching from the fist, 47; manning, 47
Turkey, 1
Turner, William, 13

U.S. Fish and Wildlife Service, 14, 20–21, 38; leg bands, 47, **47**
United States Air Force Academy, 7; Association of Graduates, 14; Athletic Association, 37; as bird repository, 33–34; Library falconry collection, 75–76; selection of falcon as mascot, 9–12, 59; Speakers Bureau, 55
United States Military Academy, 9
United States Naval Academy, 9

Vanderburgh, Betsy, **38**
Vanderburgh, Mark, **38**

Watson, Ashley, **42**
Webster, Harold M. (Hal), 12, 13–14, 15, 19, 20; *North American Falconry and Hunting Hawks,* 20, 27
Wings of Tomorrow, 13
Wood, D. P., 17
Woody, **84**

Young, Jack C., 15, 20, 23, 25
Young, Tyler, **42**

Zazworsky, John, **38**

Woody, one of the Academy's kestrel falcons, glances over his shoulder before taking off. Photo courtesy Office of the Director of Falconry, Air Force Academy.